To Raymond
& Whitey" Riker

Best always

AN AMERICAN JOURNEY

MY LIFE ON THE FIELD, IN THE AIR, AND ON THE AIR

Jerry Coleman

with

Richard Goldstein

TRIUMPH
BOOKS

Library of Congress Cataloging-in-Publication Data
Coleman, Jerry.
    An American journey : my life on the field, in the air, and on the air / Jerry Coleman with Richard Goldstein.
    p. cm.
    Includes bibliographical references.
    ISBN-13: 978-1-60078-064-6
    ISBN-10: 1-60078-064-4
    1.Coleman, Jerry. 2.Baseball players—United States—Biography. 3.Baseball players—New York (State)—New York—Biography. 4.New York Yankees (Baseball team) 5.Sportscasters—United States—Biography.I. Goldstein, Richard, 1942- II. Title.
    GV865.C6425A3 2007
    796.357092—dc22
    [B]

                                                                        2007041061

This book is available in quantity at special discounts for your group or organization. For further information, contact:

Triumph Books
542 South Dearborn Street
Suite 750
Chicago, Illinois 60605
(312) 939-3330
Fax (312) 663-3557

Printed in U.S.A.
ISBN: 978-1-60078-064-6
Design by Sue Knopf
Photos courtesy of Jerry Coleman unless otherwise indicated.

Dedication

For Maggie, Diane, Jerry, and Chelsea
–Jerry Coleman

For Nancy
–Richard Goldstein

Contents

Foreword

Mr. Dooley, the fictional Chicago saloonkeeper created by the journalist and humorist Finley Peter Dunne (1867–1936), said, "When we Americans are through with the English language, it will look as if it had been run over by a musical comedy." As proof of Mr. Dooley's prescience, consider how the word "hero" has been pounded into shapeless mush.

People commonly say that pop singers and an assortment of other celebrities living risk-free and very remunerative lives are "heroes." A few years ago a defense contractor took out newspaper ads to praise one of its products, an airplane, as "heroic." Memo to contractor: only people—and very few of them—can be heroic.

The book you are holding is by one of them.

That is not, however, because he played on eight pennant-winning Yankees teams. Rather, it is because Jerry Coleman was the only major league player to serve in combat in both World War II and the Korean War, both times as a Marine aviator, logging 120 combat missions.

Real heroes come in all shapes, sizes, colors, and dispositions, but most have one thing in common: they do not like to be called heroes. So I will not annoy Jerry Coleman, who is a friend, by saying any more about that. Instead, I want to note that for decades he has been one of the best and most beloved broadcasters.

Major league teams have 25-man rosters. The chief broadcaster is, however, a 26th man in terms of his contribution to the success of the franchise. His voice is part of the background music of life in the team's region for six months out of every 12, contributing to every fan's enjoyment of the season, and to the community's sense of, well, community.

Baseball is a strange game. The action is initiated by the defense, which has the ball as each episode in the game begins. At any moment, the defense outnumbers the offense, nine to one—or two, three, or, with the bases loaded, four. And baseball is the most observable of team games: 10 to 13 players are spread across an eye-pleasing green background on the largest field in team sports. (Well, baseball is played on the largest field in team sports not played with animals. A polo field is bigger.)

But although baseball is wonderfully observable, not everyone can be in the ballpark to observe it. It is sad but true: some people must, or at least do, allow their jobs to interfere with their baseball time. Hence the importance of broadcasting and, especially, of radio.

Radio has long been central to the enjoyment of baseball for several reasons. One is that it is difficult to watch your team on television while stuck in a traffic jam. Another reason is that radio is just right for baseball, a game made for someone capable of painting verbal pictures and narrating the step-by-step process by which a game builds to a climax.

Unlike games of flow, such as basketball and hockey, baseball is a game of episodes. In the 2,430 games that make up a baseball season, there are 21,870 innings featuring about 166,000 at-bats involving about 700,000 pitches. Through all this, there are the voices of the great broadcasters, narrating and explaining and enhancing the fans' enjoyment.

No broadcaster has earned a more affectionate following than Jerry Coleman. When you read this memoir, you will not only know why, you will join his legions of followers.

—*George Will*

Acknowledgments

My children know they have only to ask and I will do anything I can for them. Add some prodding from my wife Maggie, and I'm a goner. But for years I have resisted their appeals to write a memoir. I've always been too busy moving forward to take time to look back. When I received Richard Goldstein's proposal for a collaborative effort, I felt this might be the right time. I appreciate Richard's efforts in helping me tell my story. The skills he brought to this project as a writer on military and sports history proved to be of great value.

Special thanks go to my friend George Will for his very kind foreword, and to Bill Center, of *The San Diego Union-Tribune*, for his friendship and the support he provided throughout this process.

I'm grateful to Tom Bast, the editorial director of Triumph Books, for his guidance, enthusiasm, and patience. Adam Motin, Triumph's associate editor, ably shepherded this memoir to completion.

Paul Bresnick, our literary agent, merits many thanks for his hard work and encouragement.

Finally, I am indebted to the San Diego Padres organization and to our Padres fans for allowing me to do what I love in our beautiful city.

A Bittersweet Day

"There are only two
  important things in life:
  the people who you love
  and who love you,
  and your country."

1

A Bittersweet Day

I cannot speak for others who have returned from serving their country, but as I returned home from Korea in 1953, I felt the same rush of emotions that I had experienced following World War II.

There was a sense of relief, followed by the joy of being reunited with friends and loved ones. At the same time, I found myself dealing with the "Why?" question.

Why was I returning? Everyone who served had close buddies who didn't.

Tragedies that claimed some of my closest friends had somehow dodged me. I didn't dodge them. I wasn't that great a pilot. No one was. But God allowed some of us to return home and called others.

Returning from Korea did have a much different feel than my return from World War II. I was still a kid when World War II ended. I didn't really know what the future held. But in 1953 I was returning to a hero's welcome...which made me uneasy.

Had they let me decide how to return, I would have grabbed a glove and simply gone back to playing baseball. Instead, the Sunday afternoon of September 13, 1953, was set aside as Jerry Coleman Day at Yankee Stadium. More than 48,000 fans were there, many of them coming to welcome me back.

I had been away nearly 18 months with the Marine Corps. In Korea I had flown 63 missions in a fighter, mostly in support of ground operations for the real heroes of the war.

In World War II I had flown 57 dive-bombing missions against the Japanese in the battles for the Solomon Islands and the Philippines.

As the Yankees prepared for Jerry Coleman Day, I learned I was the only major league player to have seen combat in both wars. Honestly, I was just doing my duty. Others would have done the same thing had they been asked—or had they been able.

Jerry Coleman Day actually came three weeks after I had arrived back in San Francisco, which is also my hometown. I received my separation papers from the Marine Corps at Treasure Island. I already felt home when, on the night of August 27, I flew into LaGuardia Airport with my wife, Louise, our three-year-old daughter, Diane, and our 16-month-old son, Jerry.

The Yankees had notified the newspapers in advance of my return. We were greeted by a barrage of flashbulbs as we stood at the top of the stairs drawn up against the Trans World Airlines plane. There was a police honor guard.

I felt awkward. What I wanted to do was grab a bat and hit a baseball. I needed to play baseball again. I wasn't one much for ceremony. I was proud. I felt fortunate. But I wanted to be one of the guys again, in the clubhouse, out on the field.

A Yankees public relations man named Ed Fisher was there to greet us, and Jimmy Cannon, the *New York Post* sportswriter—best known for his "Nobody asked me, but..." columns—accompanied us in our car as we headed toward the Triborough Bridge, a motorcycle policeman leading the way.

Cannon had been a correspondent in Korea, and he was hoping I'd share some stories of the war as we headed back to the Bronx. But, as he would write in the *Post*, "What Coleman knows of combat belongs to him, and he doesn't want to part with it. All the good ones are like this, a little ashamed of talking too much about it, being careful not to dramatize it, being certain to play it down."

The Yankees were on the road, but the next day I went up to Yankee Stadium and posed for a welcome-home shot with George Weiss, the general manager. I donned my old uniform, No. 42, and Weiss held up a large photo of me. "I'm in top shape," I told the reporters, "and I may be able to do something in two weeks." Weiss was going to pay me a month's salary to close out the season, and while he was a man who hated to part with a dollar, if the thought of my sitting on the bench for two weeks bothered him, he didn't show it. We both gave it our best smiles.

I took an overnight train to Cleveland and went right from the station to Municipal Stadium, that cavernous bowl off Lake Erie, for a Saturday afternoon game with the Indians. I was reunited with Frank Crosetti, our third-base coach, who had been a Yankees shortstop for 17 seasons and was a fellow Bay Area native. Crosetti embodied the Yankees tradition and had taught me how to conduct myself the Yankees way when I first came up. Now he put me through a little workout. He tossed some pitches, and I hit a couple of them to right field.

Pretty soon I was on second base. But the game with the Indians hadn't begun. It was another "feel good" photograph. This time I sat on the bag during batting practice to oblige the photographers, with our right fielder, Hank Bauer, Crosetti, and Eddie Lopat, our superb lefty pitcher, encircling me.

I was about to rejoin the dominant ballclub in all of sports, to put on the Yankees uniform again—beside Mickey Mantle and Phil Rizzuto; Yogi Berra, Bauer, and Gene Woodling; Lopat and those other terrific starting pitchers Whitey Ford, Vic Raschi, and Allie Reynolds—and endure the lineup shuffling and once more hear the storytelling of Casey Stengel.

Four years earlier I had been named by the Associated Press as the American League's Rookie of the Year. I was playing second base for the Yankees in that summer of '49, and I hit a bases-loaded double—a blooper, but a big hit nonetheless—to finish off a wild weekend when we beat the Boston Red Sox twice at Yankee Stadium and edged them out in a thrilling pennant race. The following year I had been voted Most Valuable Player in the Yankees' World Series sweep of the Philadelphia Phillies.

Now it was time to go back to baseball and shake off the rust—as if this were just another spring training. But it was hardly so simple. I told sportswriter Jimmy Cannon, "I feel like an outsider barging in."

The Yankees were cruising toward a fifth consecutive pennant. But on my first day with the team, the Indians' Bob Lemon threw a three-hitter that Saturday afternoon before a Ladies Day (remember those?) crowd of more than 28,000 in near 100-degree temperatures.

"Not even the return of Captain Jerry Coleman, famous Marine jet pilot [actually I flew a prop plane] and Korean War hero, seemed able to rouse the Yankees," John Drebinger wrote in the next day's *New York Times.*

There it was—the phrase the sportswriters always used: "war hero."

I've always hated this idea that I was a hero, something that was written very casually in accounts of my service as a pilot in two wars. I'm indebted to Red Barber, one of baseball broadcasting's pioneers and a magnificent professional, who taught me a lot when I became his partner on Yankees games in the 1960s. But I still remember how he always wanted to lean on "the heroic Coleman." On a TV program one time, I said, "Red, you ask me a question about the military, I'm going to leave." My god, he did. I hated that. Because there were others who suffered a great deal or didn't come back.

My idea of just who qualified as a hero had hit me with an emotional jolt in that late summer of 1953, when I returned from Korea. It played out two weeks after I rejoined the team in Cleveland.

It was a few hours before the festivities began for Jerry Coleman Day in September. The Yankees were playing the Indians once more, this time at Yankee Stadium. I was staying at the Concourse Plaza Hotel, not far from the Stadium, when I got a phone call early in the morning. I was a mess to begin with. I was down to 145 pounds—I only weighed around 160 when I had been playing—and the anticipation of the ceremonies was weighing on me. The caller said, "I'm Max Harper's brother-in-law. His wife is here and would like to see you."

Major Max Harper was my roommate during the Korean War. One day on a mission deep in North Korea, he was flying the attack plane in front of my Corsair when he went down. I watched his plane crash. There was nothing I could do.

In Korea, a lot of people disappeared and were found later in prisoner-of-war camps. Max Harper's wife had been hoping he was captured. This distraught woman wanted to know whether Max was really dead. She wouldn't accept it from anyone but me. She knew I was on that mission.

We met at the hotel, and I told her, "Yes, he's dead. I saw it."

I explained the circumstances. She had a look of desperation. It was the worst look I ever saw. I guess it should have been my greatest day as a Yankee. Instead, it was turning into my worst.

Shortly before the game with the Indians began, I was running around in the clubhouse—dying slowly over the impending tribute—and Ed Fisher, the Yankee public relations man, said, "Hey, there's some Marine here who wants to see you."

I said, "Who?"

"I don't know, it's some Marine."

I thought it was one of my squadron mates, so I went out there. It was Lem Shepherd, the commandant. Well, if you don't know what the commandant of the Marine Corps looks like, you get demerits. I felt so stupid. I didn't even know who it was until I got there.

We shook hands, and General Shepherd thanked me for my service.

Then came the ceremonies, presided over by the voice of the Yankees, Mel Allen.

Admiral Bull Halsey, for whom I'd flown in World War II, said a few words and received a huge ovation. The Marine Drum and Bugle Corps and precision drill team, flown up from Washington, put on a show. Eight of my fellow pilots from Korea did a flyover. On behalf of my teammates, Allie Reynolds presented Louise and me with silver and chinaware. Just as the ceremonies were to close, a cream-colored Lincoln Capri rolled out from the left-field bullpen, a gift from the Yankee co-owners, Dan Topping and Del Webb.

And then Mel Allen led the crowd in singing "Happy Birthday." (The following day I would be 29.) Finally, Mel drew the biggest cheer of the ceremonies when he announced that "No. 42 will be at second base for the Yankees."

I was filling in for Billy Martin, who had a sore back. Up to now, I was simply working out. This would be my first time in the lineup since a previous ceremony in my honor at the Stadium on the afternoon of Sunday, April 30, 1952, when my teammates sent me off to Korea between games of a doubleheader with the St. Louis Browns.

Now, on Jerry Coleman Day 1953, the Korean War was over. The demarcation point between the two Koreas was back at the 38th parallel, where it had been when the carnage began in June 1950.

There were 200 former prisoners of war in the Yankee Stadium stands. I told the crowd, "They endured a great deal more than I ever thought of or ever did." My hat was off to them. They were the ones who should have been where I was, not me.

Everyone else seemed to have a good time on my "Day." But with all those memories flooding back, that moment with the widow of Max Harper, it was a bad day for me.

I've always said this, though it sounds corny. There are only two important things in life: the people who you love and who love you, and your country. Those are the things that are critically important to every human being.

When World War II was over, I wondered what would come next. It was almost a letdown. But when the Korean War ended, I was back with the Yankees right away, in the midst of a pennant race.

The important things you try to put in the right place, and the unimportant things you just skip by. When I got back from Korea, I was sitting on the bench and the Yankee players were running around, yelling. I couldn't get interested in it. I couldn't get into it because there were other things that I thought were more important. I was happy to be alive. I had a tough time.

If you lose 10 men, or five men, or two men, or whatever, that's more important than losing a baseball game, although you want to win the game just as much as you ever did. When you see guys die, you recognize that you're not going to live forever, even though you think you are. And we were all so young. I was 19 when I went to the Pacific in World War II to fly a Dauntless Dive Bomber. My gunner, Stretch Meenan, was 18. I kid about this, but it's true. If the Japanese knew what they were up against—meaning the two of us—they would never have surrendered. We were a couple of kids. And American kids were all over the place in World War II.

The memories of the guys I flew with in World War II and in Korea who never made it back stayed with me.

When your roommate is blown up in front of you, and he had five kids, as Max Harper did, you think differently. I remembered another flier in Korea we called Ski—he had a Russian or Eastern European name, Romaniski, or something like that—who went down. He couldn't decide whether to bail out when his plane was hit, and then it was too late. And there were others. A pilot named Phil Doty was blown up on the runway at Green Island in the Solomons when I was stationed there. His plane didn't get off the ground, and he didn't get rid of his bomb. He died and he took his gunner with him. E.E. Fryer was shot down over Luzon in the Philippines. And there were guys whose names I didn't even remember anymore.

I fought a couple of "clean wars" in the sense that you fight a "rotten war" on the ground. That's where you see all the gore and guts. In the air, people simply disappear.

Homer Gratz was a pilot from the Midwest I trained with, a good friend, newly married. He was in another squadron, in another sector of the war, in the Central Pacific, in World War II. They send you on vector searches—I hated that—an hour this way, an hour back, checking to see if there are any ships in the area. You're flying at about 100 feet because if you're looking for a ship, you see it on the horizon as the superstructure shows up. Homer's job was to check whatever vector he was searching. But he never came back. Who knows what happened to Homer? Apparently he had engine trouble.

I saw Max Harper get hit, but most of the time you don't see it happen. You go into a dive. You've got 12 planes going down. You're concentrating on the target. You come up. You've got an item peter—item point—and join up with the other fliers and go back to base. Then you realize, "Where's No. 6?" Nobody knows what happened.

There were all these guys who I knew and aren't with us anymore. You think differently. But I never talked about these things with my Yankee teammates. It's done. People who were there understand. People who weren't there would never understand.

San Francisco Memories

"Wounded by life and nearly killed by an abusive husband, my mother kept pulling her family together against overwhelming odds. I have no idea what would have become of my sister and me had it not been for her care and tenacity."

2

San Francisco Memories

San Francisco appeared as the promised land for many Depression-era Americans toward the end of the 1930s.

The Golden Gate Bridge was considered among the marvels of the modern world when it opened in 1937. And two years later, San Francisco hosted the Golden Gate Exposition, the city's version of a World's Fair. But San Francisco took a beating during the Depression. Bread lines, soup kitchens, and labor strife were a way of life. And it was a doubly agonizing time for the Coleman family.

I shouldn't have many good memories of my childhood. But I do. And the reason for that is a woman born Theresa Viola Pearl Beaudoin in 1902 in San Jose.

My mother was an amazing person. Life dealt her a harsh hand even by Depression standards. Wounded by life and nearly killed by an abusive husband, my mother kept pulling her family together against overwhelming odds. I have no idea what would have become of my sister and me had it not been for her care and tenacity.

My mom was the daughter of a carpenter from French-speaking Canada. Her mother was from Detroit and of Irish background. My mom's own childhood was altered by the death of her father when she was nine or 10 years old.

It didn't take much to make my mom happy. She always fondly remembered the piano she had as a child. I remember how she would talk about the joy of sitting in a tree and eating an apple. I have pictures of her taken during World War I when she became involved in patriotic gatherings. She was 15 or 16 at the time and dressed as Lady Liberty. She was beautiful.

In pictures, my mom is always smiling. To this day, I cry when I think of what she went through. She had a hard life. But she made it as normal as possible for my sister and me.

My father, Gerald Griffin Coleman, was one of nine children born to Irish immigrants. Although his eight brothers and sisters were born in San Francisco while my grandfather was working in the men's clothing section of a department store called the Emporium, Dad was born in Los Angeles.

My father had dreams of being a ballplayer. He had played for the Navy team at Mare Island in California during World War I as a teammate of Lefty O'Doul, who became a great major league hitter and later a San Francisco celebrity as the manager of the Pacific Coast League Seals. In 1919, my dad, who was a stocky guy of maybe 5'6", caught for the Seals and Seattle Raniers of the PCL and handled a couple pitchers, Tom Seaton and Duster Mails, who made it to the major leagues.

When Gerald Coleman and Pearl Beaudoin met, evidently on a blind date, he was working as a teller at the old Angelo Bank in San Francisco while playing for the semipro San Jose Bees in his free time. The way he told it, he was being paid more to catch for the Bees than to work at the bank—I think it was $50 a week, good money in those days, to play semipro ball—so it was worth his while to commute between San Francisco and San Jose. Pearl was working with her sister, Marie, at Woolworth's. She was in the office, and her sister was a counter waitress.

My parents were married in 1921. My father was 26, my mother 19. Soon afterward, they moved to San Francisco full time. My sister, Rosemarie, was born two years later, and then I came along on September 14, 1924. We were both born in San Jose, my mother having taken a bus back there when she about to give birth so her longtime doctor could attend to her.

We grew up in one of those typical San Francisco row houses, on 26th Avenue, close to the zoo and near the beach. The house had a garage and a stairway going up to the main floor. We had a living room, a dining room, a breakfast room, the kitchen, two bedrooms, the bathroom, and the floors were all hardwood. My parents bought it for $4,200.

My father had ambitions to be a professional baseball player, but number one, I don't think he was a very good hitter. And number two, by the time he got to San Jose, he had to have a job, so he never got beyond that brief stint in the Pacific Coast League and semipro baseball.

To a casual observer, it probably seemed like a fine childhood for my sister and me—a house, my father with a steady job—but trouble developed. My mother was wonderful. But my father was a drinker. He was not an alcoholic in the sense that he couldn't function; he always worked. But he was a mean person, especially when he got drunk.

One of the first things I remember, it was around Christmastime. I got a log-cabin set. I wanted to put it together, and he was helping me. Apparently I disrupted his train of thought or got him mad because I wanted to do it and he wanted to do it for me. He picked me up by the pants and the shirt and started swinging me around. I thought he was going to throw me right into the fireplace.

My mother was screaming, and he finally put me down. When something like that happens, you never trust a person again—and that's the way it was for me with my father. My mother finally left him when I was eight years old or so. I can't be sure, but I think he must have hit her. She moved into a one-room apartment with me and Rosemarie.

My mother loved to dance. In those days, they had dance nights at some place, I think it was called El Capitan. But my father, who was still working in a bank, evidently thought she was playing around. I guess he'd been drinking, and he got a gun. He went over to the club when she was coming out and he shot her. She was hit three or four times. She ended up in the hospital, fighting for her life.

Since my father was known around town as a ballplayer, the shooting was a front-page story. I saw the headline the next day in the *Call Bulletin*. And the morning after it happened, two reporters showed up at our apartment.

They said, "You Jerry Coleman?"

I said, "No." I don't know why, but I instinctively didn't want to identify myself. My name never got into the press.

My mother said, "I just want to be left alone" and didn't press criminal charges, and my father left town. I know that he never went to jail. He moved to a place called Susanville and worked there and played baseball.

My mother's sister Marie, who lived in San Jose, got ahold of me, and I went down there and moved in with my five cousins, all boys, who accepted me like I was the plague. Rosemarie went to live with our maternal grandmother.

Aunt Marie and my uncle put me in a Catholic school, where I wasn't a very good student. The worst time I had in my life was the summer I spent with them. My uncle was a painter, but there were no jobs during the Depression, and he had to support his wife and five kids. So we'd all trudge out to this fruit place where we'd pit apricots all day long. I can still remember, I'd pit one and eat one, pit two and eat one. That's how we spent our days. I didn't eat an apricot for years after that. Oh god, I hated them. And there were hobos living on the tracks. It was really a desperate situation for this country.

After nine months, my mother got out of the hospital, and my sister and I were reunited with her. My mother's left elbow wouldn't bend, and her left leg was crippled. She had to wear a brace that fit around her ankle so she could walk. The brace went halfway up below the knee and had a bar on the right. She wore it until the end of her days.

Once my mother left the hospital, the question became what we would do next. My mother got in touch with an organization called the San Francisco Ladies Protection and Relief Society. In January '34 one of their representatives, a woman named Georgina Hale Ash, sent a letter to her with some advice: "The little boy must not go to his father. The wisest thing for you to do would be to all go on relief for the time being. This will give you an apartment and food for the three of you. Your husband told me you would receive $20 per month from him, but of course one cannot tell how genuine this promise is.

"It is too bad you are having all this worry and strain, but it will soon be settled, we hope."

There was plenty of strain to come. We did go on relief in San Francisco, in the worst section of town. We had one room at Fillmore and Post streets. The state paid for our lodging and food. That was the only money we had. We got $4.20 a week or something like that. My mother would sit down every week and write "5¢ for peanut butter, 20¢ for two quarts of milk," a long list for whatever she could buy. But Mom made sure that she had enough money left over for my sister and me to go to the movies and for us to buy a Sunday newspaper.

Every month we would go down to this place that was for people on welfare and get a roast. It was in a package. I was to carry the roast back on the streetcar with my mother. I dropped it once and it rolled right at her feet and opened up. She must have died from mortification because everyone knew who we were and what we were—that we had this specially packaged roast because we were on welfare. I'll never forget that rolling roast.

At Christmas, my mother must have gone frantic, and someone showed up with a token gift. That to me was probably the lowest point of my life from the standpoint that we had virtually nothing except for our devotion to each other.

We got one pair of shoes a year from the welfare system, and that resulted in one of the most embarrassing things I can remember. I always ran through my pair of shoes. In San Jose, when I had spent time with my cousins, we never wore shoes anyway, but it was okay down there. But in San Francisco, running around barefoot wasn't too good. One day I had to wear my sister's Mary Janes to school. That was when my mother realized how desperate things were. The memory of going to school in my sister's shoes still burns inside me.

Meantime, my mother's brace had a spring that often broke, so I had to go to the University of California hospital to get it fixed—a very long walk that became an all-day journey. She eventually got something better, but that wasn't until the World War II years.

My father came back to San Francisco in 1935, two years or so after the shooting. My mother had divorced him, but because our situation was so desperate, with my mother and my sister and I living in this squalor, and because he had a job—he was working for the post office then—she married him again. There wasn't any ceremony. It was probably at a clerk's office since they were still married in the eyes of the Catholic Church.

After that we moved, and I went through junior high and high school. It was more normal, but it was never normal at our house, obviously. My sister and I don't recall any talk in our house over the years about what my father had done to my mother. And I don't recall us sitting around and saying, "Isn't this awful?" It was a closed subject.

My father was working nights then—4:00 PM to midnight—and my sister and I never saw him much. He had already left for work when we got home from school, and we had left for school before he got up each morning.

For my parents, it was an arrangement more than a love marriage. How can you love a guy who shot you? My father would go through drinking spells. Once, when I was in high school, we were in the kitchen. I thought he was going to hit my mother and I stood up and stared at him. I was 5'10" or 5'11" by then, maybe a half-foot taller than he was. He backed off.

He was an angry, angry person. I don't know what his problem was. When I was in elementary school, I always thought that people knew who I was and what I was doing because of the terrible experiences of my life. I thought people were whispering "There's Jerry Coleman," and pointing me out. They weren't, of course, but I always felt I had to be in the shadows. I didn't get over that for years, literally for years.

I don't remember discussing this with anyone, not even Father Meehan, our family priest. I was ashamed. It was like a black mark.

My mother was a very religious person. That's probably what got her through the disaster. My mother was even afraid to tell my father she was suffering from glaucoma. I think she didn't want to upset him, so she didn't properly take care of it. She would pray. And every Sunday, she went to church. I reluctantly went to catechism on Saturdays.

Soon after my father came back, we moved again. I was going to junior high school then, about a two-hour walk from home. I used to leave at 6:00 every morning. Later, I took a streetcar that cost a nickel. The students got a card. For a dollar, you got 25 rides or so. When you got on the streetcar, they'd punch the ticket until the card was used up.

I did have some good fortune. Twice I was hit by automobiles and emerged with barely a scratch. Once I was out in the neighborhood someplace and then I woke up in a doctor's office. Apparently I had walked in front of a car and it knocked me out, and these poor frantic people in the vehicle were beside themselves. They took me to the doctor, then drove me home to my mother. Later, when I was on the way to junior high, I stepped off the curb and some guy in a car shot across the street, hit me, and knocked me about 20 feet down the road. Books went flying, everything went flying. I just picked myself up, grabbed my books, got on the streetcar, and left.

If my father could have made $200 a month working for the post office, we'd have been in heaven. I think he was making $150 a month or so. So there wasn't a lot of money floating around. But it was amazing how far a dime could go in those days. A good movie was a dime, the cheap ones were a nickel. I loved going to the Liberty Theater on Fillmore Street and the Golden Gate Theater. I think I saw *Snow White*, one of the first movies Walt Disney made, at the Golden Gate. I loved Warner Oland as Charlie Chan and cowboy movies.

And a dime would buy you a hot dog, a piece of pie, and a drink. The only problem was, I didn't have many dimes. I'd have a nickel and I'd try to bargain for the hot dog and either the drink or the pie.

I was part of a group that loved to play. We were known as the Scott Street Wimpies. There were five of us: Joe, Dick, Phil, Billy, and myself. We'd show up at the Golden Gate School playground every day. Give us a game, any game...marbles, hide-and-seek, tag, ball.

Playing ball was the best. And we'd use anything we could find for a bat and ball. The bat could be a broomstick or an old shovel handle. The ball might actually be an old beaten-up ball. Or it could be some old socks wound up with tape.

Every now and then, we'd break a school window while on the playground. It's funny when I look back on those broken windows because they taught me some valuable lessons. If you told the truth about how the windows were broken, they'd let you go and the window would be fixed in a day or two. But if you didn't fess up, they'd hunt you down, and the window would sit there broken until the mystery was solved. The guilt would grow and grow.

I went on to Lowell High School, housed in a building known as the Old Brickpile, at Hayes and Masonic in the Haight-Ashbury section, only four blocks from our flat. Lowell was founded in 1856, on Powell Street between Clay and Sacramento, as the first public high school in California. It had long been known as the best high school in San Francisco and a premier school in the state for sending students to college. It still has a wonderful reputation. You would be stunned at the number of successful people who came out of there. J.D. Salinger and Carol Channing went to Lowell around the time I was there; Pat Brown, who became governor of California; Supreme Court justice Stephen Breyer; and the sculptor Alexander Calder were all Lowell graduates.

To get in, you had to be academically qualified or be a jock, and that's what I was. My junior high school basketball coach, Harry Amey, knew Benny Neff, the basketball coach at Lowell, so they found a way to get me in, though I was a neighborhood kid as well.

I had a job selling magazines and newspapers. That was all through junior high school and the first year of high school. I'd knock on every door in the neighborhood and ask if they'd want to buy a *Liberty Magazine* or a *Saturday Evening Post*. But I kept going back to the same places that didn't want them. I could've improved my marketing, but I wasn't thinking that way.

My sister was a marvelous student, and she took care of my mother when there was a problem. My parents eventually moved out to 10th Avenue in the Sunset neighborhood, a block and a half from Golden Gate Park. That's where my father had a heart attack and died in 1961 at age 66. Four years later my sister moved with my mother to San Jose.

My mother had a stroke in her eighties, and for her last seven years she was in a chair—she could think, but she couldn't move. She only had use of her right arm, and the stroke magnified the complications from her old gunshot wounds. She couldn't feed herself. My sister was an angel. She retired from her bank job—she was a secretary and then a loan officer at Wells Fargo—to be our mother's nurse. When my mother died, she was nearly 90 and virtually blind from glaucoma.

Looking back on this, on all the tragedy, it made me think that people are concerned with so many superficial things in life.

I never really used my family situation as an excuse. My fears that people knew what happened to me, to my family, would linger, but I tried to just pass right by that stuff, to focus on what was next.

I was not a good student. I thought if I threw on my baseball or basketball shoes at school, that's all I had to do. I certainly wasn't dumb, but I didn't know you had to study. It was the education that I had at the table with my mother and sister that got me over the top. My mother would regularly give me English lessons.

The two things that saved me were my mother and then my athletic ability. I was always good at sports. It gave me a presence that I would never have had otherwise. My mother was my greatest booster. She was my guiding light. She never gave up on me. She was it and there was nobody else. She was incredible.

My mother had such uncommon strength considering what had happened to her. What a lousy life. The only thing she had were her kids. She had a great daughter and a son. And I never heard a word from her of "poor me." As my sister once put it, "She was a strong lady. She never let the past take over."

Up from the Sandlots

"All of the sudden from the back of the hall walked in two naval aviators.... Not too many people flew in those days, but I took one look and said, 'That's what I want to do.'"

3

Up from the Sandlots

I can still recall the first night baseball game I ever saw. It was at Seals Stadium in San Francisco, probably in the late 1930s, when I was beginning high school. I never saw anything so green in my life. It was just like someone had opened my eyes to the world. I said, "Oh, my god, isn't that beautiful."

Lou Gehrig was my favorite player as a youngster. My mother bought me a book about his life. But Joe DiMaggio was the great player in San Francisco with the Pacific Coast League's Seals when I was growing up, and the city's large Italian population took special pride in him—he was the son of an Italian immigrant fisherman.

I never saw him play in Seals Stadium, but I can remember when he had his consecutive-game hitting streak going in '41 with the Yankees. It was incredible. He was a god, an icon beyond belief. He was always on the front page in the San Francisco papers. Every day the buzz around town was, "Did he get a hit? Did he get a hit?" Of course, his brothers played in San Francisco, too, first Vince and then Dom, whom I did get to see play at Seals Stadium. Dom became a great center fielder with the Red Sox but carried one fatal sin in life—his name was DiMaggio. He was always overshadowed by Joe.

We used to listen to the Seals' play-by-play man, Ernie Smith, on the radio. The Seals had "ball days" for the youngsters, where kids got in for free. They'd get on this tower and throw balls out into a massive group of fans, and you'd try to scramble for the ball and put one in your pocket.

My first organized team was in Catholic Youth Organization base-ball at Holy Cross Church when I was in the sixth or seventh grade, and I did some pitching. We played at Ewing Field, which was a terrible dirt lot littered with junk. I think they also played soccer on it. The bases were stone blocks. When you ran to first base, you'd hit a big rock, then another big one at second base, and again at third, if you made it that far. I don't recall what they used for home plate.

Sandlot baseball at the Big Rec ballfield in Golden Gate Park was my home away from home. That's where I spent all of my summer days. There was a man by the name of Anson Orr who gave me a regulation glove for my birthday. To this day, that's one of the greatest gifts anyone has ever given me. Gold was not as important. I'll never forget that glove. I cherished it, I slept with it. I never had a glove before that, and this was a regulation one like professional players used. I can still see that thing. It was dark brown.

Anson Orr was just an old man who loved baseball—he died a few years later—and he liked me. I was 12 or 13, in junior high school. A lot of times he brought the guys to his house, which was a block away, and fed us lunch. In those days if you went to the drugstore for a bite, you'd get a milkshake and a hamburger or a hot dog for 15¢. Garnering that 15¢ was a major challenge. So Mr. Orr kept us alive through the day, giving us the energy to play baseball with those lunches.

In the ninth grade at Roosevelt Junior High School I went out for the baseball team, thinking I would play the infield. But the catcher broke his hand the first week, and they made a catcher out of me. I could throw—I could always throw. A guy could swing at the ball and miss, and I could catch it. I could keep my eye on the ball while a lot of the kids might put their heads down and slap at it while closing their eyes.

I also took part in CYO track meets. I won the dash in my first year of competition and the dash and broad jump the second year, but they disqualified me from the broad jump because I wasn't supposed to be in two events.

When I entered Lowell High School, I played basketball and I was an infielder on the baseball team. As a junior, I made the second team in basketball; I wasn't a starter until my senior year. Our basketball coach, Benny Neff, did a marvelous job. Later he coached at St. Mary's College. He was an intense guy. He grabbed me by the hair on my head one day and said, "You go over here." There was one kid on the team, a bright fellow named Bob Arnold, who mixed it up with Benny in the gymnasium, actually started to punch him. Benny was very aggressive and maybe not as calm and relaxed as you should be at that level, but he had a winning record for a long time.

I was playing for Lowell when I got my first newspaper credit for baseball, in a column on high school athletes written by Bob Stevens of the *San Francisco Chronicle*. He was summarizing each team and he said, "Coleman, good prospect." A semi-headline. *Oh, wow*, I thought, *that was just sensational!*

But my best sport at Lowell was basketball. I was an all-city player. Bob Stevens, in breathless prose, told of my tying a San Francisco high school single-game scoring record: "Wheeling around guards that seemed to melt before his masterful feints and pivots, slender Jerry Coleman nailed himself a share of the city scoring standard yesterday in Kezar Pavilion, pouring home 23 points as Lowell conquered Commerce, 38–21. The handsome rhythmic Lowell forward left a wake of embarrassed defenders behind him, catching cold in the draft created by Jerry's artful pivots that sent him whirling 'neath the backboard."

Twenty-three points may not sound like much for a record-setting effort, but the game was played on March 8, 1942—run-and-gun basketball was far off.

My scoring feat notwithstanding, I was plenty impressed with another basketball player, someone I would meet again seven years later on an October afternoon at Yankee Stadium.

Our Lowell team was facing the Stanford University freshmen, and UCLA was playing the Stanford varsity in the regular game. After our game was over we sat and watched, and a guy on UCLA was the star of the main game. I was thinking, *Oh wow, this guy is incredible*. He was everywhere. He danced all over the place. You could not help but notice him. That was the first time I saw Jackie Robinson.

While I was playing baseball and basketball at Lowell I also played on a sandlot baseball team called the Keneally Yankees. A fellow named Neil Keneally, who owned a bar at 14th and Valencia, even though he didn't drink, supported the team and supplied the bats.

Joe Devine was a key Yankees scout on the West Coast back then, along with Bill Essick; Paul Krichell, another great scout, covered the East Coast for the Yanks. In the 1920s Devine had signed Joe Cronin out of San Francisco for the Pittsburgh Pirates, and he was responsible, along with Essick, for getting Joe DiMaggio for the Yankees. Anybody coming out of the Bay Area who was any good, Devine wanted him and got him.

Devine introduced himself to me one day. He said, "I'd like to know if you'd like to play for the Keneally Yankees."

I said, "I can't. I just signed up for the A. Romeo fish company." There was a night league they were setting up. A. Romeo had a big red-and-blue fish across the front of the team jerseys, and I thought that was rather classic. The next year, as soon as I finished playing for the fish company, I went over to the Keneally Yankees and stayed with them through my high school days while I was also playing baseball for Lowell.

Keneally got the cream of the crop in San Francisco. Bobby Brown, a lifelong friend who went on to become a Yankees teammate and later became a cardiologist and then the American League president, was on the Keneally team. So was Charlie Silvera, who broke in with me in the minor leagues and became a backup to Yogi Berra. Dino Restelli, later an outfielder for the Pittsburgh Pirates, was also on the team. Of course, nobody with Keneally had any idea what the future held for them. We were just a bunch of kids. They'd gather us at the bar and drive across the bay and sometimes all over the peninsula for our games.

And in those days, semipro baseball was huge in the Bay Area. They had night leagues and Sunday leagues, and on Monday you'd see literally hundreds of box scores in the newspapers.

My mother never missed a game—baseball or basketball—while I was in junior high and high school, and my sister also came to my games. My father went to some, but by then he was working the 4:00-to-midnight shift at the post office.

But what my mother had wanted me to do, and what I wanted to do, was go to college after I graduated from Lowell in June 1942. The University of Southern California was the big sports school on the West Coast. Benny Neff at Lowell knew Sam Barry, the baseball and basketball coach for USC, and they arranged for me to get me a combination baseball and basketball scholarship.

The Brooklyn Dodgers were interested in me early in my senior year at Lowell. Ted McGrew, the chief Dodgers scout, wanted to sign me. The Dodgers' scouts came in after the 1941 World Series, when the Yankees beat them in five games, and they had a tryout camp at San Mateo. So the guys on the Keneally team all went down for workouts, and the Dodgers were going to offer me a contract on the spot.

I recall it vividly. I was in this room, and Tom Greenwade, who later became a Yankees scout and signed Mickey Mantle, was there, and also Jake Pitler, who became the Dodgers' first-base coach after the war. They were giving me the big pitch about signing. My dad was all for it. I think about $2,500 was the deal, which was huge—people didn't have any money. But I wouldn't sign. I said, "I'll have to talk to Joe Devine." He was back in New York at the time, having been at the World Series.

Then came a Sunday when I was playing in a semipro baseball game at Alameda. They stopped everything around the third or fourth inning. Someone announced that the Japanese had bombed Pearl Harbor.

That ended my plans to attend USC. The war had started, and nothing was important except the war. No matter what you were doing, for kids 17 years old, the questions were: What am I going to be? What branch of the service am I going to go into? All of us wanted to do something to support our country, to join the military.

One day in March 1942, the principal at Lowell High School asked all of the senior boys to come to the auditorium. We were sitting there wondering what was going to happen. All of a sudden from the back of the hall in walked two naval aviators whose gold wings were about four feet wide from my looking at it, and they told us about the V-5 program, which trained naval aviators to get their gold wings. Not too many people flew in those days, but I took one look and said, "That's what I want to do."

But you had to be 18 years old to get into the program, and I wasn't going to be 18 until the following September. I had to fill the summer in some way, and I didn't want to be a warehouse man or something like that, so I figured I'll play pro baseball while waiting for a chance to become a navy flier.

Having put off accepting that Brooklyn Dodgers offer, I caught up with the Yankees' Joe Devine. He was a father figure to me. All the advice that I got for my future came from him. And the Yankees were the sports team of the world so far as San Francisco went because of DiMaggio, and before him, Tony Lazzeri, Lefty Gomez, and Frank Crosetti, all Bay Area boys.

Joe Devine was a wonderful person. This is getting ahead of things, but years later he protected me in contract negotiations with George Weiss. In 1946, when I got out of the Marine Corps, the Yankees sent me a contract for $125 a month. I was making $260 in the Marines, for heaven's sake. So I battled and battled with Weiss, and Joe Devine got me a contract for, I think, $300 a month. And the next year I went through the same machinations and I ended up getting $500 a month to play for six months. Joe's the guy who got me that deal. He really did.

Anyway, I wasn't exactly idle in the winter of 1942. I was pretty enterprising. I worked for a kosher meatpacking firm in San Francisco that had a baseball team I played on. I had a job at the slaughterhouse. They would run the steers through these very narrow lanes. They had to knock a steer out first, then they'd shackle him up on his hind legs and cut his throat. There was a guy in charge there named Sam. He said, "Hey, you wanna knock one?" The idea was to hit the steer over the head with this thing, like a sledgehammer, right between the eyes, knock him out and cut his throat. It was a very sanitary way and easy for the steer. I figured it was going to die anyway, so I'd give it a shot. I tried it. I hit the damn thing in the eye. It was a mess. Sam had to come in and finish it off. That was the only one I ever tried. It didn't appeal to me much.

Joe Devine eventually arranged for the Yankees to give me $2,800 to sign with their minor league organization. I gave the money to my mother for whatever she wanted. She got a refrigerator for the first time—no more icebox—and something else that told a lot about what lay ahead for me and so many others: war bonds.

Two days after I graduated from high school, I headed off to join the Wellsville Yankees of the Pony League, short for Pennsylvania-Ontario-New York, where the teams were from. This was Class D ball, the lowest level in the minors and one step up from high school level.

Two of my buddies from the San Francisco sandlots and high schools, Charlie Silvera, the future Yankees catcher, and Bob Cherry, had been signed as well, and we took a train together to Chicago, then changed trains for the rest of the trip.

Wellsville, New York, was a town of 5,200 in the Genesee Valley, around 160 miles from the Hall of Fame in Cooperstown. Of course, I was hardly thinking about being inducted into the Hall one day.

We had an eventful episode when our train passed through Warren, Ohio. Somebody jumped in front of the train and committed suicide. The train stopped, and we were bogged down for a long time. Finally, one of us said, "Let's go back and take a look." We jumped off the train and were about 100 yards away when it started to leave. So we ran after it—three lunatics from California trying to catch a moving train. We did get back on.

We got to Wellsville around midnight or 1:00 in the morning, and then the train pulled out and the lights in the station went out. So here we were in some place we didn't know anything about, everything pitch black. We went down to the main street, and there was a hotel—Pop's Pickup Hotel. How do you like that name? We walked in, these three loonies from nowhere not knowing what to do. But we got a room. They had blowing fans on the wall. I turned one on. It wasn't covered, and it nicked the tip of my index finger and put a nice crease in it.

The next day we found our way into wherever the offices were for the baseball team and told them, "We're here." They put us in the stands for a couple of nights to watch the games. We thought, *Oh, man, we're going to tear this league apart.* We tore it apart to the point where I struck out in my first six at-bats over two games.

When we played at Batavia, New York, I finally got on first base. The pitcher hit me in the ribs in the middle of a beanball battle. I could hardly hold a baseball for my first three weeks at Wellsville because of that run-in with the hotel fan, but eventually I played better.

Charlie, Bob, and I later shared a large upper room—three beds—at a home at 120 Maple Avenue. They had a big porch in the front, and that's where I read *Gone With the Wind* while waiting for the night games.

The man who owned the Wellsville team had a daughter, Jane Dixon. She was 21 and I was only 17, but I fell in love with her. There was nothing sexual about it. I loved her because her family had the biggest refrigerator in town and she took care of us. She'd tell us "come on over" and we'd raid the refrigerator on a daily basis. I was making only $75 a month. And she used to take the three of us out to the lake to go swimming. We had a wonderful time.

We had an all-dirt infield at Tuller Field, the Wellsville ballpark. One day, when I showed up for practice, I noticed a long, lean man with sort of swarthy skin and steel hair. He was raking up pebbles, making little piles, putting them in a wheelbarrow, and running them off—a part-time groundskeeper.

I guess he'd been watching the games while he was doing this job. He came up to me and said, "You know how to hit-and-run?"

"No," I said.

"Wanna learn?"

"Sure."

"Be here at 10:00 tomorrow morning."

So the next morning I showed up. He said, "When I throw the ball, you hit it, wherever it is. Because on a hit-and-run, you must make contact."

So he'd throw it high and low and say, "Hit the ball, hit it." And we kept going and going. And finally, he got me where I could make contact and hit the ball wherever it was thrown. And then one day he didn't show up. I went to Wellsville's general manager and I said, "Whatever happened to that man who was helping me with my hitting?"

He said, "Oh, you mean Chief Bender."

Chief Bender, a Chippewa Indian, was one of the greatest pitchers of all time, a star with Connie Mack's championship Philadelphia Athletics teams early in the 20th century. He pitched in five World Series and he's in the Hall of Fame. He was known as Mack's "money pitcher."

Chief Bender taught me things that I used my entire career. He had me choking up and hitting the ball behind the runner, learning how to make contact. I think that George Weiss had given him that groundskeeping job. He evidently didn't have any other job, and it was just a way to make some money. I never saw him again.

Sometimes, preparing the infield was mostly a do-it-yourself project, as a longtime Wellsville resident named Paul Ryan once recalled in a *Baseball Digest* article: "I went down to a game in '42 one night. I remember it had been raining a lot that day and the field was in bad shape. I looked out on the field and there was the groundskeeper and two players out there working on the field, trying to get it in shape. The two players were Charlie Silvera and Jerry Coleman: they had what it takes."

Kids like Charlie and me were forever coming and going in that vast Yankees farm system. Don Ludden, the last general manager for the Wellsville team before the franchise left town in 1965, remembered it for *Baseball Digest* this way: "We were always at odds with the major league team. We'd get a good player and they'd move him up to a better class of baseball. When the Yankees had the farm team here in the 1940s, there was one year when we had 75 players go through. It seemed like every train that came in would have two guys with suitcases getting on and two getting off. Finally some of the fans hung a sign on the gate of Tuller Field where we played that said, 'New York Yankee Experimental Station.'"

Over the years I stayed in touch with Jane Dixon, the Wellsville girl with the wonderful refrigerator. When I was in the Marine Corps during World War II, I'd send her a note and she'd send me a note. Maybe eight to 10 years ago, somebody came up to me in Atlanta, where I was broadcasting a game with the Padres, and said, "Do you remember Jane Dixon?"

I said, "Sure, how's she doing?"

"Well, she's downstairs. She wants to say hello."

So down I went, and here was this white-haired woman who could hardly see. And I thought, *Oh, my god.* She was just a neat young lady when I met her my first year in pro baseball. She was very shy about the whole thing in Atlanta, and I think she felt badly because physically she wasn't well. It brought back some wonderful memories, but it was also very sad.

In October 2006 I took my wife Maggie on a trip to my baseball past to mark our 25th wedding anniversary. We visited the minor league towns of upstate New York, beginning with Wellsville, where a 17-year-old kid waiting to go to war got off a train in the middle of the night in the summer of 1942.

The Wellsville diner was still there, and I remembered the woman who had served me a steak dinner and all the trimmings and dessert for a dollar. Tuller Field was still there. The home where I boarded with a family was still there, now a rooming house. And the train station was still there. It had become a national landmark, though they hadn't fixed it up yet. The "Wellsville" sign was hanging, a bit askew.

Five thousand people back in '42, still 5,000 people more than six decades later. So much had changed—for the world, for me—and yet so much had stayed the same in that little town on the Genesee River where it all began.

Going to War

"Any veteran will tell you that war can play cruel tricks with your mind. But the worst of times produced some of my fondest memories."

4

Going to War

Early in September 1942, with my season at Wellsville over, I returned to San Francisco and went down to the ferry building, where they were accepting applications for the navy's V-5 preflight program. The line snaked all the way up to Nob Hill.

I went through the physical and mental tests, which weren't so hard. It was practical stuff, multiple choice, A-B-C-D. The final part was being interviewed by a commander who wore three bars and looked like Admiral Perry. He got to my high school transcript, which was not one of the great transcripts of all time. He frowned and said, "I can't sign this."

I said, "I beg your pardon, sir?"

He said, "You know how much it costs to train a naval aviator?" I had no clue, of course. "It costs $300,000. You're going to get halfway through the program and fail."

My high school transcript was a C average at best, but I must have been a good salesman. He said, "You'll never make it, but you passed everything. I have to sign this."

I wanted to prove to that guy that he was wrong. All through the program, I got very good grades—I was in the top echelon both mentally and physically.

My first stop for training was at Adams State Teachers College in Alamosa, Colorado, where we were going to school and learning to fly. It was freezing weather. But what I remember most was that I was up against men from the University of California and Stanford who were supposedly smarter than me, but I found I could compete with those guys. A lot of them flunked out. I was just a high school kid, 18 years old, but I began to get some confidence in myself.

I was a little heavy on the pedals, but finally my flight instructor cleared me to fly solo. I'll never forget it. When the plane left the ground, I thought, *How in the hell am I going to get this thing down?* I had a grand total of eight hours of instruction.

But I made it, and from Alamosa I went to St. Mary's preflight school in California. Some great athletes were there—Frankie Albert and Norm Standlee from the football world, and Hank Luisetti, who popularized the one-handed shot in basketball. They served as physical training instructors.

An unforgettable moment was when Joe Foss, the war's celebrated Marine air ace, spoke to us at St. Mary's while touring the country to sell war bonds, spur military recruiting, and inspire war-plant workers. Flying a Wildcat fighter that was slower than the Japanese Zeros, Foss had shot down 26 fighters and bombers in the battle for Guadalcanal from October 1942 to February 1943. He had become the first American pilot of World War II to equal Captain Eddie Rickenbacker's record in World War I, and he came home to a hero's welcome. President Roosevelt had invited him to the White House and had given him the Medal of Honor. I wanted to be Joe Foss Jr. I was trained by the navy, but I had set my sights on becoming a Marine aviator. My romantic ambition was to sink a Japanese aircraft carrier.

A little later I went to Olathe, Kansas, and flew the "yellow peril," a training plane with bi-wings. I almost killed myself when I was there. When you finished your flying program for the day, you'd go up to the adjoining fields and pick up corpsmen and bring them back. And all of a sudden there was one of those awful Midwestern storms showing up. I landed and looked at this storm in the background that was heading toward me, and I thought, *I'd better get the hell out of here.*

Instead of going on an L-turn to get to this guy, I cut across the field in high gear, and I overlooked a big hole in the ground. I hit it, and the next thing I knew I was upside down. Then the rainstorm finally hit. I just dropped out and ran over to a hut and waited for the storm to pass. They were looking to get rid of people right and left—if you washed out, you became a seaman second class. My career didn't look too good at that point, but my instructor saved me. He felt that I was going to be a good pilot and stood up for me, and they left me in.

From there I went to Corpus Christi, Texas, and flew the Vultee Vibrator, which was a low-wing monoplane, and then I went through the instrument phase and advanced flying.

Colonel Richard Mangrum, who had led one of the first two Marine squadrons to fly into Guadalcanal early in the battle for the Solomons, was at Corpus Christi, interviewing the fliers who wanted to be in the Marines. Mangrum had been a pilot at the Ewa base near Pearl Harbor when the Japanese attacked, destroying Marine dive-bombers on the ground. But he got back at the Japanese when he arrived on Guadalcanal in '42.

Mangrum sat me down at Corpus Christi and said to me, "Why do you want to be a Marine?" He scared the daylights out of me, and I don't remember what I said, but he okayed me, and I became a Marine student. When I graduated and was commissioned an officer on April 1, 1944—April Fools' Day—instead of being an ensign in the navy, I became a second lieutenant in the Marine Corps.

From there it was on to Jacksonville, Florida, where I picked up the SBD—the Dauntless dive-bomber—for operational training. My best friend from San Francisco, Bob Cherry, who had played with me at Wellsville and had gone through pilot training with me, also chose the Marines. He went to Jacksonville with a fighter group, and I went there with a dive-bomber group and became qualified to fly off aircraft carriers. I requested dive-bombers because they were the kind of planes that might sink a carrier.

On May 7, 1942, during the Battle of the Coral Sea, Lieutenant Commander Robert Dixon, the leader of the navy's Scouting Squadron 2, reported that his dive-bombers sank the Japanese carrier *Shoho* by radioing the memorable words, "Scratch one flat-top."

The Dauntless dive-bombers piloted by navy fliers dealt the Japanese a huge blow in the Battle of Midway on June 4, 1942—a turning point in the Pacific war—when they sank the Japanese carriers *Akagi*, *Kaga*, *Soryu*, and *Hiryu*.

Most people think of the Marines as the "grunts," the men who fought storied battles at Belleau Wood in World War I, Iwo Jima and Okinawa in World War II, the Chosin Reservoir in Korea, and Khe Sanh in Vietnam. When you talk about military aviation, people think of the air force and maybe the navy. But Marine aviation goes back to 1911 when Alfred Cunningham, a lieutenant at the Marine barracks in Philadelphia, attempted to get an aerial contraption into the air by bouncing it off a ramp at the Philadelphia Navy Yard. He didn't leave the ground that time, but on August 1, 1912, he soloed after almost three hours of instruction at Marblehead, Massachusetts, becoming the first Marine aviator.

In World War I two Marines flying a De Havilland DH-4, Lieutenant Ralph Talbot, the pilot, and Corporal Robert Robinson, his gunner, received the Medal of Honor for repulsing 12 German fighters that jumped them, knocking down two.

The idea of dive-bombing goes back to 1919, when it was first carried out by a Marine lieutenant, Lawson H.M. Sanderson, during the occupation of Haiti. In an interview for a Marine oral history project, Sanderson described how he thought up the concept one night while he was in bed at his Quantico barracks. He improvised a mail bag to serve as his bomb rack, and the release mechanism was a rope from the bag's mouth to his cockpit. He put his Jenny plane into a 45-degree dive and yanked the rope that opened the mail bag to send the bomb off. The Marines and the navy ultimately found that dive-bombing was more accurate than horizontal bombing.

Early in World War II Marine pilots like Joe Foss, Pappy Boyington, and Marion Carl gained renown for shooting down Japanese planes in the battle for Guadalcanal and the campaign that followed in the Solomons.

Apart from these legendary exploits, and the perfection of dive-bombing, a lot of guys were killed in aerial training during World War II. A lot of crazy things happened. One night in Jacksonville, our leader took us on a dive-bombing practice run, and we were peeling off and heading in. And then I heard on the radio, "Break it off, break it off. Pull right." There were some other planes coming at us from the other side, doing the same target. There were planes all over the sky—it was incredible. We could have had a midair collision easily.

In the middle of the summer in '44 they sent me to Cherry Point, North Carolina, where it was hotter than sin with mosquitoes every-where. We were jumping into a river, pretending we were commandos. It was a basic training thing more for the Marine ground than the air, but they wanted us to get a feel for what was going on.

There were probably several hundred pilots trying to get the hell out of there and into combat. They were ferrying planes out of Cherry Point, going from one part of the country to another.

One day, about two weeks into the three-week program, they lined us up. "The following officers step forward. Gerald F. Coleman, 036103..." About five of us stepped forward. I thought, *My god, they're going to shoot us.* But they said, "You're going to Miramar." They ran us out to Miramar Naval Air Station in California and from there to El Toro, which was just north of Miramar. Soon I was on my way to the Pacific, aboard a troopship heading to Guadalcanal. I got D deck, which was the lowest deck, and everybody down there was sick for the entire 20-day trip. It was the most atrocious time I ever had.

I was assigned to VMSB-341—a Marine scout bombing squadron. We were known as the Torrid Turtles. There was a picture on the side of our planes of a turtle carrying bombs. The other squadrons in our group had somewhat fiercer names like Black Panthers, Sons of Satan, Wild Horses, Flying Goldbricks, and Bombing Banshees. How the name Torrid Turtles came to be remains a mystery to me.

Guadalcanal was a staging area, and in the late summer of '44 I flew out of Henderson Field, the first airstrip of any consequence in the Pacific captured by the Marines. You had to have four hours a month to get your flight pay—that was $75 a month beyond your base pay of $150. So I made a couple of flights just to pick up flight time.

I used to take a walk every day. While I was out on one of my walks, they attached several of us to a squadron that would be flying out of Green Island, a coral speck in the Solomons that had a runway and not much else. When I got back from the walk, they had all taken off on a plane to Bougainville for processing and instruction en route to Green Island. Since I missed the plane, I had to go there on an LCI, a flat-bottomed boat with a ramp that was used to ferry troops onto the beaches in the island-hopping campaign. It was up and down all the way to Bougainville, and I was seasick for three days.

My squadron was a part of Marine Air Group 24, whose operations officer, Lieutenant Colonel Keith McCutcheon, organized 40 lectures for 500 pilots and gunners on the theory and practice of close air support. And he arranged joint training exercises with the army's 37th Infantry Division on Bougainville.

When I finally got to Green Island, I began flying raids in the Solomons with the Dauntless dive-bomber. Douglas Aircraft built more than 5,900 of them between 1935 and 1944. They were spectacular planes for accuracy. You could hit something very easily. They weren't fast, though, and you'd get to 10,000 feet and you'd about had it. Rabaul was a huge air base for the Japanese, and Kaviang was another base. We ran a few missions in and out of there.

The war in the Solomons was winding down when I got there, but most places were not totally secure. There were Japanese holdouts on Guadalcanal and Bougainville. When I think of taking those walks by myself on Guadalcanal, I must have been insane because enemy soldiers could have been in the hills or in the bushes or anyplace.

We'd have briefings—usually the night before a mission—where they'd tell you the target, the hour to take off, and when to join up with the other planes. There were usually four on a mission. The briefers pointed out all the artillery and anti-aircraft stuff you could expect—guns over here and guns over there—and maybe they'd all be shooting at you. So it was nerve-wracking even before you got into the air.

Predawn takeoffs were tough because you were finding your fellow fliers in near-dark conditions. And if you returned at night there weren't a lot of lights at the base, and you had to find the runway. All our runways were Marston Matting—steel things that looked like waffles. No cement; they just laid them out in a hurry.

With the dive-bombers, you'd be going straight down, doing 280 or 300 knots. We would release our bombs at 1,500 feet, then get down to 500 feet and be on our way. We'd open up the flaps, which were perforated. If you didn't open them up, you'd pick up a lot of speed. It happened to me once. I thought they were open, but they weren't.

I looked and said, "Holy cow." I was probably going 100 knots faster than I should have. Either the flaps didn't open because of some mechanical problem or I simply forgot to open them. I got out of it okay, but I got down way too low.

In dive-bombing, accuracy is critical. If you were going too fast, you wouldn't have the same accuracy. Not that I'm bragging, but I was never totally off target to where I'd be bombing indiscriminately. If you were on a mission and you couldn't drop your bombs, oftentimes they didn't want you to come home with them. They'd want you to drop them in the ocean or something, because if you had an accident, you'd blow up the base.

When we weren't dive-bombing—we usually carried 1,000-pounders or 500-pound bombs—they had us on strafing runs. The Dauntless had two .50-caliber machine guns up front that fired from the moving propeller, but that was very little firepower.

I kept the same gunner all through the war—Patrick Meenan from Tyrone, Northern Ireland, a lanky 6'2" or so whom I called Stretch. He had come to America as a baby with his mother, their father having arrived before them, and he grew up in Manhattan, one of six children. He had left Cardinal Hayes High School to join the Marines, trained at Parris Island, and then found his way into the aviation section. He was the bravest man in the Marine Corps, so far as I was concerned, because he put his life in my hands every time we took off. If I made a mistake, he'd be dead, too. I've always thought about the poor gunners in the back. They had no control over anything.

In the Dauntless, the gunner sat in the rear, his two .30 caliber machine guns facing upward. Stretch was very careful with his ammunition boxes. The briefers had told him that if Japanese planes hovering in the vicinity or the enemy on the ground had seen a bunch of ammo boxes being discarded from an American dive-bomber, they would figure the gunner was probably out of ammo and could fire away at will. So he would keep those ammo boxes in the plane after they were used up or make sure not to expend ammo carelessly.

In the Solomons, when you came back from a mission, you were over water all the time. If you went down, you'd have to get in your raft and hope someone would find you before the Japanese did.

Any veteran will tell you that war can play cruel tricks with your mind. But the worst of times produced some of my fondest memories.

I remember New Year's Eve of 1945. Late in 1944 we had been moved by ship from the Solomons to the Philippines, where we were going to fly close air support as General MacArthur fulfilled his "I shall return" pledge.

We landed just before New Year's Eve and two fellow pilots, Bob Means and Bud Madden, commissioned me to get us dates for the night. Now I don't know what the ratio of men to women was where we were stationed, but 1,000-to-one might be a conservative figure. But with the first call I made, I found three nurses who didn't have dates for New Year's Eve. That should have told me something.

Bud, Bob, and I found this Jeep and headed out to get our dates. It goes without saying that we were surprised. I had just turned 20. My date, Flora, was at least twice my age and size. During the evening, the other two nurses went to the bathroom and never came back. Flora stayed with me.

After the traditional New Year's Eve kiss, I jumped into the Jeep and headed back to camp. All was cool until the next morning when I learned I had jumped into the wrong Jeep and returned to quarters with the base commander's wheels, which were now parked just outside my door.

We spent New Year's Day alternately laughing and trying to figure out how to get the Jeep back to where it belonged without getting caught. Eventually, someone came to claim it without ever saying a word.

As for memories of my date, I named my plane after her...*Florabelle*.

Sadly, it was too soon back to the business of war. In January of 1945 the army staged the Lingayen Gulf invasion, which was the beginning of the battle for Luzon Island and Manila.

I got to Lingayen Gulf three days after the invasion began. We came in on little boats, and the Seabees were still working on a runway. We waited to bring the planes in. The more senior pilots in time overseas were flying in.

We were living in tents in a rice field. One day I heard a *bump, bump, bump,* and I looked up and there were two Japanese Zeros coming at us. Talk about guys scrambling. We had these bamboo jugs of water.

I ran into one and almost knocked myself out. We all jumped into the same foxhole. At night it was almost like a circus when the Japanese planes would come in. Shrapnel and tracers were going in all directions. A couple of guys were out of their foxholes watching, and a bomb killed all three of them. Another night, in Zamboanga, near the end of my time in the Philippines, some Japanese sneaked inside our base and chopped up half a dozen guys—slit their throats in the tents.

We had begun dive-bombing missions on Luzon at the end of January '45, and after one month our Marine pilots had dropped more than 200,000 pounds of bombs. We had 168 Dauntless dive-bombers in there. We supported the army troops and we also did deep interdiction strikes, hitting Japanese troop positions all the way up to Apari in northern Luzon, often on patrols with six planes or so.

On one mission to Apari, the pilots returned when it was dark. One guy thought the runway was in a particular spot, but what he had seen was actually the area where planes were parked. He plowed into them and blew up six planes and himself at the same time.

Our missions were often in flurries. When the Luzon peninsula was being taken, we were on call all the time. You'd just sit around and wait and then it was "We need you," and you'd run out and hop in your plane.

The little mosquito planes would spot our target from the air. The Japanese would never touch a mosquito plane. Once they did, they would expose themselves. The mosquitoes were at 1,500 feet; our dive-bombers were at 10,000 feet. The mosquito planes would tell the artillery units at the front to drop shells with white phosphorus at whatever coordinates they had. And you'd be circling above and pick it up. One of the problems was the wind. Sometimes the wind would blow that white phosphorus away and you'd have trouble finding your target. You had to be careful. Sometimes pilots made critical mistakes—bombed their own troops—though it didn't happen with my squadron.

When you were doing deep interdiction, say, 200 miles into enemy territory, you didn't have the mosquito planes as spotters and the artillery to fire the white phosphorus shells. Pathfinder planes would drop the phosphorus for you, which was not an easy job since they didn't have coordinates from the artillery. To make sure you hit the right target, they would go in first, and we'd be right behind them.

I remember a particular mission around Davao, I think. We were coming back with eight planes, and I noticed some blinking on the ground. I was the only one who saw it. I called my flight leader and I said, "Major, I think I'm getting some mirror flashes off the ground. You want me to check it out?" Airmen were given a mirror. If you held it in a certain way at the sun and moved it at a certain angle, you'd hit whatever target you wanted to hit. They were hitting me.

The major sent another plane with me. We went down, skimmed right over the top of them. If we circled, any Japanese in the area could see what we were doing. There were two or three guys standing in the water, at the edge of land, frantically waving T-shirts or whatever. There were maybe six or eight of them. I think a couple of them had been injured. Their PBJ, the navy version of the B-25 Mitchell bomber, had evidently been shot down.

It was Japanese-held territory, but I couldn't tell just how far they were from Japanese troops. We called in a flying boat, the PBY, that rescued the guys an hour or two later. They sent us a case of beer and thanked us profusely, but I never met any of them.

The close air support of our troops on the front, which was vital, gave you a fair chance to survive if you were hit because you could bail out and hope that someone would rescue you. But if you got caught deep in Japanese territory bombing their troops, you were done—there was no way you could get out of there.

When we had hit our targets, all the planes on a particular mission would join up at a predetermined altitude—say, 3,000 feet—circle around, and then go home. And that's when you'd ask, "Where's Bill?" Someone might be missing, and you had no idea what happened to him.

But the Japanese air arm was almost nil at that time. They were pretty much out of it, so there were no dogfights that I knew of. What we were concerned with was anti-aircraft, the ack-ack stuff that could get you. We lost a couple of guys who were shot down. On a mission I flew over Baguio, a big parcel of land went flying just a few feet in front of me. Apparently, the guy flying ahead of me had hit an ammo dump, and I was almost nailed by part of the debris. Baguio was where General Yamashita, the head of the Japanese army that had conquered the Philippines, had his headquarters with 10,000 men. They all slipped away before our troops took control of the city, but in September '45 Yamashita came back to Baguio to sign the unconditional surrender of the Japanese army in the Philippines.

There were plenty of close calls. Once we were on a mission—16 planes—and all of a sudden a huge front came through. I'll give credit to our skipper: he found a dirt runway. There was mud all over the place but we all got in safely.

And in Davao, I got a glimpse of General Stilwell, a renowned figure from the fighting in Burma.

One of the tragedies of the Philippines came when our planes were flying from Lingayen Gulf to establish our base at Zamboanga in the south. A dive-bomber had an engine problem off Panay Island and had to land. A small airstrip there at a place called San Jose had supposedly been cleared of Japanese. It was "friendly," according to intelligence reports. So the pilot and his gunner landed there and they waved to one of our transport planes that had seen them touch down. But the military had made a mistake: the intelligence was wrong, and the airfield wasn't cleared of Japanese. The men were captured. When we eventually took control of the airstrip, they were found buried nearby. They had been beheaded. It could have happened to any of us. We were always warned that life was cheap if you were captured. You could expect harsh treatment, if you survived captivity at all.

But I never let the prospect of an emotional blow over losing a buddy keep me from friendships with the other pilots. I didn't drink, so I didn't spend a lot of time at the club at night. I was kind of removed from that group. But this aside, I was close to the other fliers.

I shared a tent in the Philippines with three other pilots. One of them, Bud Madden, was on Stanford's NCAA basketball championship team of 1941-42. He was the sixth or seventh player into the games. Madden used to call me Jack Armstrong, the All-American boy, because I was always running around and doing things, playing baseball and basketball when we had a little free time. Another of my tent mates, Bob Means, was a terrific pilot, an instructor at Jacksonville when I went through there. The third guy was Art Mauer. They were first lieutenants, and I was a second lieutenant, so I got all the dirty jobs.

There wasn't much contact with home. Often we didn't get mail for weeks. One time, a plane had our squadron mail and found us on this Liberty ship going from the Solomons to the Philippines. But the plane dropped all the mail in the water. I can't remember if we ever got it. Now you get a computer and you can talk to your wife every night from Iraq. Of course, Tokyo Rose was on the air all the time, talking to us, if you had a radio.

Our outgoing mail was censored. Anything that mentioned your location, you marked out or cut out with scissors. I did censoring myself; all officers had that task.

My mother once sent me a salami. It was all mildewed by the time I received it, and I threw it away. I didn't realize that I could have washed the mildew off and cut it open. I thought it was rotten but it was still good.

I remember one time when we had a few days off, I went with Bud Madden and Bob Means to Manila. We drove down at night to find nurses, I guess. Somebody said, "Hey, here's some good prewar rum." I put aside my distaste for alcohol and had a glass. I was deathly ill for three days. I was hanging out of the Jeep upchucking all the way back.

In July 1945 all pilots qualified to fly off aircraft carriers—I was one of them—were called back to the States. We were to pick up carriers and hit the Japanese mainland in November, or at least that was the rumor.

I flew from the Philippines to Guam to Kwajalein to Johnston Island and finally to Hawaii. When we got there, we thought, *Hey, this is really great*, but they had a curfew. You had to be off the streets by 5:00 PM, so we didn't do much socializing.

I went home to San Francisco after flying 57 missions in the Solomons and the Philippines.

The final leg of my trip back to the States was carried off in style, thanks to my tentmate Bud Madden. I don't know how he did it, but he got three of us on Pan Am's China Clipper with sleeping accommodations. We ended up there with admirals, generals, and senators, so I didn't feel too comfortable as a second lieutenant. We had a Class 2 priority to get back—Class 1 was the top. We finally landed in San Francisco, and I said, "This is really neat."

When they brought the China Clipper in, they attached a rope to the stern and to the bow and towed it in sideways. Unfortunately, one of the lines broke, and we floated back into the Bay. Here we're gone a year, we're getting home, and I was never more frustrated in my life. Finally, about two and a half hours later, they pulled us in.

Then I got a leave. A month later, we dropped the atomic bombs on Hiroshima and Nagasaki, and I never did get to fly off an aircraft carrier. V-J Day had finally arrived.

But I wasn't quite out of the Marine Corps. Sometime during my leave, when the war was over, I got a call from the Miramar air station saying, "You've been transferred to Cherry Point." I told them, "I live in San Francisco. I don't want to go to Cherry Point." But they said, "Lieutenant, you're going to Cherry Point. Your orders are on the way."

When I got to North Carolina—I had already been there during training—they put me in the SB2C, which might have been the worst plane I ever flew. It was called a Hell Diver, but it was a death trap. It really was a very dangerous, lousy plane—big, bulky, unpredictable, hard to control, engine problems—and no one who ever flew it liked it. A lot of navy pilots did fly it. It had great armaments—it had four 20s up front—and you could carry 2,000 pounds of bombs. It was really a tremendous offensive plane, but there were so many problems with it. If you were in a dive with an SBD, you could recover quickly if you were a little off balance and were strung out. You could come back with it. An SB2C, you're done. You'd better stay on target all the way down. In my last three months in the service I was checked out on them, but finally in January 1946 I received my discharge from the Marine Corps. The war was over and now I would have to decide what I would do with the rest of my life.

If I continued my quest to play professional baseball, I would be facing stiff competition. Hundreds of prewar ballplayers would be returning from military service.

By December 1944, 41 men who had played minor league baseball before the war lost their lives. Perhaps the most highly publicized minor leaguer in combat had been Billy Southworth Jr., the son of the St. Louis Cardinals' manager. An outfielder for the Toronto Maple Leafs of the International League, he became the first man in organized baseball to enlist when he joined the Army Air Corps in December 1940. A B-17 Flying Fortress pilot, he flew 25 bombing runs over Europe. But in February 1945, shortly after he took off from Mitchel Field on Long Island for a flight to Florida, an engine on his B-29 Superfortress failed and he crashed into Flushing Bay. He died at age 27.

John Pinder, a one-time right-handed pitcher in the minors, received the Medal of Honor posthumously for his actions at Omaha Beach in the D-Day invasion. An enlisted man in the First Infantry Division, he was hit while bringing radio equipment ashore but made additional trips to the beachhead in waist-deep water before dying of his wounds.

Nobody on a major league roster at the time of the Pearl Harbor attack died in action during the war. But two men who appeared briefly in the majors in 1939 were killed. Elmer Gedeon, who played five games in the outfield for the Washington Senators, died in April 1944 when the plane he was piloting was shot down by a German fighter over St. Pol, France, five days after his 27th birthday. Harry O'Neill, who caught one game for the Philadelphia Athletics, died on Iwo Jima in March 1945.

And there were others from the sports world who lost their lives. Nile Kinnick, an Iowa back who won the 1939 Heisman Trophy, became a navy pilot. He died when his plane went into the sea on a training mission off the aircraft carrier *Lexington* in June 1943. Jack Lummus, an end for the NFL's New York Giants, serving as a lieutenant with the Fifth Marine Division on Iwo Jima, was awarded a posthumous Medal of Honor for a one-man assault on Japanese positions after being wounded by hand grenades.

They call the World War II veterans the greatest generation. But in my opinion, every generation is the greatest generation. When this country is threatened, people rise and stand together. How about the people in the Revolutionary War who gave up their homes and everything to create a country? We don't think enough about that. After 9/11 the country came together. When it's called upon, every generation will meet the challenge.

The Road to Yankee Stadium

"The first time I stepped on the field, it was like being in a cathedral. At second base, when you looked up, it seemed as if you were looking at the Empire State Building."

5

The Road to Yankee Stadium

A few months after my discharge from the Marines I was back in the state of New York playing baseball again, but I had left Wellsville of the Pony League behind. The Yankees promoted me to their Binghamton Triplets farm team in the Eastern League.

Lefty Gomez, the Yankees' great pitcher of the 1930s and a future Hall of Famer, was the manager. Lefty had a reputation as a colorful character and a storyteller, and he was a fun guy to be around. He was very warm to the players, but he wasn't destined to be a manager. It was just a job he needed at the time, so George Weiss hired him.

I had one run-in of sorts with Lefty, but it was just a misunderstanding that I can laugh about now. They had these camp followers around at Binghamton, as they had in any baseball town. One day, before a doubleheader, there was a knock on the door of the hotel room I shared with another player. These two girls walked in. Believe me, nothing untoward happened. All of a sudden, in walks Lefty. I said, "Lefty, it's not what you think." He told me and my roommate, "You're both fined $25." I was making about $300 a month.

Long afterward, he used to tease me about it when I saw him at banquets. His strength was public relations and selling—he did promotional work for Wilson Sporting Goods for many years—and he was in demand as an after-dinner speaker.

Our 1946 Binghamton team lost 89 games, which is still a record for the Eastern League, and in Lefty's second and last season, the Triplets lost 88 games. At times, we must have seemed like the baseball version of the Keystone Kops.

Bobby Bragan, a longtime baseball man, once recalled a weird episode at Binghamton in an interview with the *Dallas Morning News*, reflecting on his career:

> Gomez had a catcher who wasn't too sharp. He never could recognize other players, only by their numbers. Binghamton is finally leading a game in the bottom of the ninth, and a runner tries to score the tying run from second. He slides, jumps up, and runs to the dugout. But the umpire hasn't given a sign. So Lefty hollers to the catcher that the runner has missed the base, so run and tag him. By then, the runner had reached the dugout and sat down, and the catcher didn't know one player from another. So he tagged a guy and looked at the ump, who didn't give a sign. Then he'd tag the next guy on the bench and so forth.
>
> The runner saw what he was doing, so before the catcher got to him, he jumped up and started running back to home plate. By then, the pitcher was standing at home so the catcher threw the ball to him. Suddenly they get the guy in a rundown. Might be the only time in history a runner got in a rundown between home plate and the dugout.

There were certainly some amusing times with Lefty Gomez at Binghamton, but I have one memory that isn't so pleasant.

Of course, 1946 was the year when Jackie Robinson broke baseball's color barrier, playing for the Dodgers' farm club at Montreal in the International League. (Jackie went on to beat out Bobby Brown, my sandlot buddy from San Francisco, for the batting title. Bobby once told me, "If they'd have given me two more weeks, I'd have had him.")

The Yankees had sent a pitcher down to Binghamton from their Newark Bears of the International League. I can't remember his name, but he was a redneck from South Carolina. He told us about how he had tried, with no success, to bean Jackie. He said, "I had to get that n— in the head. I couldn't get that n—." Growing up in California, we never thought like that. I've never thought that way, period. In fact, one day when I was managing the San Diego Padres, I had eight African Americans in the lineup. Who's the best player? That's all I cared about.

I did well enough at Binghamton to earn a promotion in 1947 to the Kansas City Blues, the Yankees' American Association farm team. Hank Bauer and Cliff Mapes, later my teammates playing the outfield for the Yankees, were on that club. There was also a fellow hardly anyone has heard of, but he figured in a heartwarming episode.

He was a pitcher named Carl DeRose, and he had a sore arm. But in June he threw the first perfect game in American Association history, beating the Minneapolis Millers in Kansas City. The fans were so appreciative that they sent him checks ranging from 25¢ to $250. A check for a grand total of $2,005 was presented to him at a ballpark ceremony. The news of DeRose's feat had even reached General Eisenhower, who sent him a dollar and wrote a congratulatory note on it.

In my year with the Blues, I learned what baseball was all about from Billy Meyer, who was the first real manager I had. Billy was a marvelous teacher, and I learned more about baseball strategy from him than any other manager I ever had except Casey Stengel.

Billy was a wonderful tactician and motivator. I remember how near the end of the '47 season, we were scrapping and scrambling to win the American Association pennant. He called a team meeting and he said, "Some of you guys are not paying attention." He read the riot act to us. He said, "If you want to win, bear down and do it right." And we went on to win that pennant. We needed that talk. He wasn't pointing a finger at me, though, as one of the carousers. I had a young wife—I had married Louise Leighton, a fellow graduate of Lowell High School, in 1946—and I wasn't a drinker or a party guy.

Billy was a baseball lifer who had never fulfilled his ambition to manage in the major leagues. But he got his chance a year later, with the Pittsburgh Pirates, and he would have Ralph Kiner in his prime— the highlight of Billy's life. Billy, in fact, got a preview of Kiner just before we opened our '47 season. The Pirates came into Kansas City on a barnstorming tour, returning from spring training, and Kiner was taking batting practice. He was hitting balls over the left-field wall like it was a hundred feet away. Meyer went "humph, humph" and shook his head every time Kiner hit the ball.

Many people have seen Billy Meyer's image without even realizing it, if they know Billy's name at all. He's the short, stubby guy wearing the Pittsburgh Pirate uniform in the Norman Rockwell painting *Tough Call*, also known as *Three Umpires*, that appeared on the April 23, 1949, cover of the *Saturday Evening Post*. It shows Billy and Clyde Sukeforth, a coach for the Brooklyn Dodgers, alongside the umpires, Larry Goetz, Beans Reardon, and Lou Jorda, who are trying to decide whether to call a game at Ebbets Field as the raindrops come down. (The Dodgers' manager at the time, Burt Shotton, wore a business suit in the dugout, so he never came onto the field.) In the painting, the Pirates are leading 1–0 in the sixth, and Sukeforth is pointing with glee toward a patch of clear sky, suggesting that the rain will soon stop, giving the Dodgers a chance to catch up. Billy Meyer never made it to the Hall of Fame, but the painting did—it hangs in the Cooperstown art collection.

When I finished the 1947 season, I hardly seemed to have the strength to make it at a higher level in baseball, let alone crack the mighty Yankees lineup. I weighed only 147 pounds because I'd smoke and I'd drink—Pepsi, orange juice—but I didn't eat very much.

After the season, I went to a doctor and I said, "I can't keep my weight up." I'd start at 162 pounds or so and go down from there. He said, "Drink two beers every day."

I said, "Doctor, I'm an athlete, I don't drink." That might have seemed strange to him, since athletes were hardly known to stay away from alcohol. But the doctor insisted. So I starting drinking beer, and I never lost an ounce after that during a baseball season. But I couldn't stand beer. It made me hiccup and burp.

I went to spring training with the Yankees in 1948, and I was the last man cut by manager Bucky Harris. I had been playing mostly at third base and shortstop in the minors, but when spring camp ended, they sent me to Newark to become a second baseman because they felt that George Stirnweiss, their second baseman, was on the way out.

Bill Skiff was the Newark Bears' manager, one of those people who worked in the minor leagues for the Yankees forever, as Billy Meyer did before he managed the Pirates. Skiff had managed in the Pacific Coast League before coming to Newark. He was a Triple A manager who had never had the big league shot and he was in his first year managing the Bears.

The first day of the season they put me at second base, but somebody took me out with a slide and hit my leg so badly I was out for two weeks. I took cold ice sprays to get my knee in shape, and when I got back, they put me at third base, where I'd played a lot. And then I went to shortstop, and finally in the last 10 or 12 games of the season, I played at second base, where I was supposed to be playing all season long.

The thing that always fascinates me in looking back was, why would they put a guy who weighs 160 pounds at third base? That's a power position, and with my power, I'd hit the ball and it would go 200 feet. I could play third base, I had a good arm, I had the defensive skills, but I should have been a shortstop and second baseman from day one and never left that spot. Every time I went someplace in the Yankees chain, there had been a shortstop or a second baseman already holding down those spots.

I had a bad year at Newark; I hit only .250. And the surroundings weren't so great either. Ruppert Stadium was a dump. It was an old ballpark, and the Yankees organization wasn't spending money to fix it up. We weren't drawing crowds of any size since so many fans were at the local taverns where they could find a TV set to watch the few major league games that were being carried back then. And my commute to the park wasn't much fun. I lived in Orange and took a bus to Ruppert Stadium that made about 47 stops.

When my season was coming to a close, Bill Skiff said, "Jerry, do you want to get to the big leagues?" I said, "Yes, sir." And he said, "The first thing you have to learn is to use your bat, have bat control—hit and run, bunt, maneuver the ball." No one knows how to do it today. It's unfortunate. It's a great way. First and third, less than two outs, you start the runner, something I eventually learned to do quite well. And I also learned to bunt well.

Except for that brief tutelage from Chief Bender at Wellsville, Skiff was the first one who taught me how to use my bat, how to hit-and-run. At the time, it didn't seem like a great idea. For the Yankees in those days, the glamour came from power hitting. You had DiMaggio, and before him Ruth and Gehrig. Everyone who came up in the Yankees chain wanted to be a power hitter. In the original Yankee Stadium, it was 457 feet to left center. It was stupid for me—a 160-pounder—to even think about hitting home runs there. So I could see that Skiff was right.

The Yankees called me up for the last few weeks of the 1948 season. The first time I stepped on the field, it was like being in a cathedral. At second base, when you looked up, it seemed as if you were looking at the Empire State Building. The Stadium, with those three decks, was huge, especially when you were in the infield. But you had to divorce yourself from that during the game because it was intimidating. For some guys, the Stadium was too imposing. They couldn't play there.

I was thrilled to be dressing alongside the great Joe DiMaggio, and figures like Tommy Henrich, the guy whom Mel Allen would christen Old Reliable; Phil Rizzuto at shortstop; and a terrific starting pitching combo of Vic Raschi, Allie Reynolds, Eddie Lopat, and Tommy Byrne, with Joe Page in relief.

But the ballclub that would dominate the American League for the next 15 years was only coming into shape. Yogi Berra was just 23 years old, catching part time and playing the outfield as well. Hank Bauer played in only a few games in '48, and Gene Woodling was in the minors. Mickey Mantle was a teenager in Commerce, Oklahoma. And Casey Stengel was managing at Oakland in the Pacific Coast League. Bucky Harris, the "boy wonder" shortstop/manager of the Washington Senators' world champions in 1924—when he was 27 years old, and the year I was born—was in his second season as the Yankees' manager.

We played the Red Sox in Boston for our final two games of the season. If we had beaten them both times, we would have finished in a tie for first place with the Cleveland Indians. But the Red Sox beat us twice, then lost to Cleveland in a one-game playoff, the first time the American League ever had a playoff for the pennant.

With TV in its infancy, the Indians had drawn more than 2.6 million fans to Municipal Stadium in that summer of 1948. Bill Veeck, the Indians' owner, had created a stir with his promotional schemes and his signing of Negro League pitching legend Satchel Paige. And after years of going nowhere, the Indians were finally atop the league with solid pitching—Bob Feller, Bob Lemon, and the rookie left-hander Gene Bearden. Larry Doby, who had broken the American League color barrier the year before, became a .300 hitter playing the outfield, and second baseman Joe Gordon, traded from the Yankees, along with the Indians' player/manager Lou Boudreau, were an outstanding double-play combination.

In looking back, one of the great frustrations of my life is that Joe Gordon is not in the Hall of Fame. He was the American League's Most Valuable Player with the 1942 Yankees, a pennant-winning ballclub that had stars, and he hit 253 career home runs, playing seven of his seasons at Yankee Stadium, where it was short down the lines but spacious everywhere else. He and Boudreau probably did as well as any double-play combination ever did in 1948. Boudreau had no range, but he had great hands and knew where to play hitters. Nobody matched Gordon that I can think of as a second baseman. The only one I know of might have been Robbie Alomar years later.

I never got into a game at the end of '48. I took infield practice, then I sat and watched. And what I saw convinced me that Bill Skiff had been right about bat control. Bobby Brown, who had already made it to the Yankees playing third base, choked up about two inches, three inches, even though he weighed maybe 25 pounds more than I did. He had better bat control than I had. Instead of swinging from the heels, he was popping the ball around.

I thought, *Gee, I'm kind of stupid, trying to hit home runs.* And that's when I started to choke up. And I learned to use the bat as a weapon. I had always swung on the end of the bat. I was swinging my tail off to try to hit home runs, and they were knocking the bat out of my hands inside.

In the winter of '48, I went home and had somebody put lead in the barrel of a bat, and I choked up on it and swung that every morning and afternoon for a half hour all winter long. It gave me a quicker bat and better control.

When I set out for spring training with Louise in 1949, I had $300 in my pocket and no car. We hitched a ride from San Francisco to St. Petersburg with Clarence Marshall, a backup pitcher for the Yankees. You talk about being stupid and nuts and full of optimism—I was just that. But the car ride seemed to take forever. We were someplace in Texas when there was a huge flood and we had to turn around and backtrack half a day to get out of the area. By the time we got to Florida, I had about $150 left. We got a little room out on the beach. I'd hustle rides with people all the time. Somebody drove Louise to New York to wait and see whether I would make the team.

When I arrived at spring training, I could hit for an hour with no problem, thanks to my wintertime workouts with the leaded bat. DiMaggio's hands had blisters, and all the other guys who had been sitting around during the winter had them, too. Back then, the players got into shape in spring training when they should have been in shape all year long. Now, because of the money, the players recognize they've got to stay in condition to maintain those million-dollar salaries and they can also afford to have those specialized trainers. We never had that.

I figured I wasn't going to make the club because I hit only .250 at Newark. And I was mostly a shortstop/third baseman. I wasn't going to take Rizzuto's job and I wasn't enough of a power hitter to play at third. As for second base, I still didn't know how to pivot correctly. That's why I got hit trying to make a double play early in the '48 season at Newark.

But one day during spring training, Joe Trimble, a sportswriter for the *New York Daily News,* came up to me with a baseball and said, "Here, sign this."

I said, "What's that?"

He said, "This is for the players on the team."

That's how I found out I had made the club.

In looking back at my year with the Newark Bears before becoming a Yankee, I'm grateful to Bill Skiff for teaching me bat control, but that's not the only thing I have to thank him for. It was probably not even the most important thing he told me.

The second thing I had to do, Skiff said, was to quit smoking. You know how romantic smoking was in the late 1930s and '40s. Every movie had some guy smoking a cigarette, maybe two in his mouth, lighting one for himself and one for his girlfriend. In the movies, they were smoking their heads off. When I was overseas with the Marines in 1944 and '45, I thought, *Boy, I'm going to learn to smoke.* I wanted to be attractive to women, of course. That was the way to do it, the charming way. It took me six months to learn to smoke a cigarette, and I said, "Ah, I finally did it."

So I started smoking and I continued to smoke. Finally, in 1948, Bill Skiff told me, "You're too small to smoke. It takes your strength away." You know how long it took me to quit? Ten seconds. I never smoked another cigarette.

When I came up to the Yankees to stay in '49, most of the guys smoked. DiMaggio, Berra, and Bauer smoked between innings. They'd go into the runway behind the dugout. Tommy Henrich was a cigar smoker in addition to cigarettes. And many of the guys chewed tobacco. By quitting smoking, I maintained my weight and kept my energy level up, and my first year in the major leagues would be better than my last year in the minor leagues.

When I stopped smoking, I immediately felt better. I didn't know what it was doing to me. The man who really saved my life in many ways—got me to the big leagues and also, who knows, might have saved my life from the standpoint of living and dying by telling me to cut out smoking—was Bill Skiff.

Becoming a Yankee

"The Yankees were our religion—to be a Yankee to me was the greatest thing ever put on this earth."

6

Becoming a Yankee

When we opened the '49 season at the Stadium against the Washington Senators, the Yankees mystique was on full display. Before the game, they unveiled a monument to Babe Ruth, who had died the previous winter. Babe's widow, Claire, and his daughters, Dorothy and Julia, were on hand. The monument was actually on the field, in deepest center, alongside plaques to Lou Gehrig and Miller Huggins. Now, of course, there are many more plaques, but they're in Monument Park behind the left-field wall.

The man who had succeeded Babe Ruth as the Yankees' living legend, so to speak, was on the bench instead of in pinstripes on that day. Joe DiMaggio was wearing a business suit and a camel hair coat, something that Ruth used to sport, since Joe was nowhere near ready to play—he was still suffering from bone spurs in his right heel. When he would be back in the lineup, nobody knew. But on this day, he wasn't missed. Tommy Henrich hit a homer in the ninth inning to win the opener 3–2.

I was sitting on the bench, just as I had been in those last weeks of the '48 season, when I was called up from the Newark Bears. George Stirnweiss, a college football star at North Carolina years earlier and a fast man on the bases, was still the starting second baseman. George, or Snuffy as they called him, had been playing for the Yankees since the war, and had won the American League batting title in 1945, though he hit only .309.

But Stirnweiss was spiked in the hand making a play on Opening Day. He finished the game but couldn't play the next day, and in fact he was out of the starting lineup for an extended period. So I got my chance, starting at second base alongside Phil Rizzuto at short. But the first ball hit to me went right through my legs into right field. Fortunately, the next batter hit a one-hop shot to me, we turned it into a double play, and I was saved.

Stirnweiss was never antagonistic toward me. I thought he was a delightful guy. There wasn't that infighting that people think there might have been. He helped teach me to turn the double play. I learned how to "catch the ball, throw the ball, and jump." Don't worry in which direction your feet are moving. Never mind going over the bag or behind the bag.

George was one of those guys who lost his skills quickly. Some people go slowly, some lose it overnight. He had a backup role for much of the '49 season, then he was traded to the St. Louis Browns the next year. He played a while for the Indians, then he was gone from the majors. He later took over the *New York Journal-American*'s sandlot baseball program. George had a tragic death. He was killed in September 1958 when a New Jersey commuter train he was riding in plunged through an open section of a lift bridge and went into Newark Bay. Around 50 people died in the accident. He was 39 years old and had six kids. Phil Rizzuto and I went to the funeral mass.

Speaking of Rizzuto, there are few men who ever set a better example of how to play the game and live life. As a player, he was very bright and never missed a ball at shortstop. Long before scouting reports, Phil was a master at preparation and positioning himself for every play. I learned so much just by watching Rizzuto. And Rizzuto's lessons could be applied off the field. Phil did things the right way. I always thought it was wrong that the Dodgers' Pee Wee Reese went into the Hall of Fame before Rizzuto. Phil was a leader on nine World Series teams. Rizzuto eventually was voted into the Hall of Fame—but it should have happened much sooner.

When I started out with the Yankees, I found that base runners were pretty tough going into second base. We had an outfielder named Johnny Lindell who was a terrific practical joker, a funny guy in the clubhouse. But he was no fun for the middle infielders.

Johnny was about 6'5" and 220 pounds. Nellie Fox, the little second baseman who eventually made the Hall of Fame, was an outstanding hitter, but he couldn't pivot well. Fox is remembered today for teaming up with a fellow Hall of Famer, Luis Aparicio, a great, great shortstop with the Go-Go White Sox, who won Chicago a pennant in 1959 after the Yankees had won four straight. But Nellie broke in with the Philadelphia Athletics. One time Lindell knocked him into left field at Shibe Park with a rough slide that broke up a double play. It was one of the worst sequences I ever saw in terms of a roughhouse play. But nobody said anything.

The base runners' game plan back then was to get you if they could. In those days the runners could chase after infielders to break up a double play. It wasn't a thing where the runner had to go to the base to knock down a shortstop or a second baseman with a slide. They could go after the guy. Today Lindell would be out for interference on a play like that one. You cannot attack the shortstop or second baseman the way they did back in the '40s and '50s.

Elmer Valo, an outfielder for the Athletics, would tell me, "I'm going to get you," but he never did. I'd tell him, "You missed again." I got nailed a couple of times, but never bad, and I still made the plays. I was never afraid of getting hit, so I found that the pivot was very simple.

I think my greatest strength was that I was quick off the ball defensively. I didn't watch the ball. When it was hit, I went with it. Whether the ball was hit to my right or left, I was moving with the crack of the bat. It was a reaction thing. Casey Stengel was asked at one time who was the quickest he ever saw, and he said, "Coleman." In fact, Stengel put me down as his all-time Yankee second baseman.

But there was a conscious, mental part, too. You've got to make sure you get within range of the bag. Every time there's a hitter and a runner, you've got to know who's hitting, who's running, and you've got to cheat accordingly so you can get to the bag when it's hit to the left side—to third base or shortstop. As I watch today, when the ball's hit, a lot of players look at it and they go. Whether it was the reaction in the brain, or in my body or eyes, my greatest strength was moving toward the ball.

I had decent hands, although I was erratic at times, and that's one reason why I was better at second base and third base than I was at shortstop. At shortstop you have to catch everything cleanly. I'd boot the ball from time to time. If I did it at second or third, I could recover and make the play at first.

At second base you should always have a flat glove because you have to get the ball out quick. It's a backward position. You can't let the ball bury itself in there like a shortstop can because you're moving toward it all the time. My glove was a Lonny Frey model. I loved it, a great glove. Lonny was with the Yankees as a backup in the late '40s, near the end of his career. He was a pretty good ballplayer. I used the same glove for two years. The third year it started to get flimsy so I got another one. Nowadays I think the glove makers give players as many as they want.

I had a good arm for quickness and for power. When we had those relays from that deep outfield at Yankee Stadium—it was 461 feet to dead center—I was the guy who made the longest throw to the plate among the infielders. Rizzuto had a quick arm but not a strong one.

The guy who became my mentor with the Yankees was Frank Crosetti. He took a liking to me and Bobby Brown. We used to go out early, before practice. He taught us the Yankee way, the image of the Yankees, and technique at the plate as well as in the field. He showed me how to bunt, how to hit-and-run, how to do things most people don't think about today. Today, if you lay down a sacrifice bunt, you get a gold star. In those days it was a normal part of the game.

Crosetti was an old-school guy. He hated it if you caught the ball one-handed, something everybody does now. One day, when we were in the middle of infield practice—most teams don't have it today, I don't know why—I said to Rizzuto, "Let's give Frank a real highlight." So we started one-handing the ball, slapping it around. Crosetti said, "Oh, wise guys, wise guys." He dropped his bat and left us on the field in front of 50,000 people.

If you didn't play the game right—step in front of the ball and make it hit you in the chest, catch the ball with two hands, make sure your throws were proper—you'd hear from Crosetti. You had to do all exacting things the way he wanted you to do them. Of course, in Crosetti's playing days, it was pretty hard to catch one-handed. He played with something that looked like those little gloves that train motormen wore.

Beyond technique, Crosetti taught me something important. He used to say, "Never give up and never give in." And in baseball, it's easy to give in, because being good is very difficult. No other sport in the history of man gives 30 percent great credit. In basketball, if you made 30 percent of your free throws, they'd shoot you. In football, if a quarterback completed 30 percent of his passes, he wouldn't make the team. You make 30 percent as a hitter—you bat .300—you're a star.

It's a very hard game in the field as well. People don't realize what goes into some of the plays that are made. They'll say, "Oh, wow." But what happened in between to get to that ball is difficult. Fielding bad hops—people don't realize how tough that is. And there's the mental part. Say some guy is pitching a perfect game—I was there when Don Larsen threw one in the 1956 World Series. The pressure's on the pitcher—right? But what about the fielders, what if they make an error? You feel the same tense disappointment if you blow the perfect game, if you don't get to a ball you should get to, and they give the guy a hit. Everybody gets involved in those kinds of situations.

When I got to the Yankees, I wasn't anywhere near a great hitter. But I didn't miss the ball—I struck out only once every 10 at-bats in my rookie season, and for my entire career as well, which isn't bad. But I didn't have power. I always kid people. I say, when I hit the ball, all the outfielders ran in and said, "I got it." When you don't have power, you've got to find other ways to help the team.

I could bunt, I could hit the ball behind the runner. I could make contact. And when I played for Stengel, Bobby Brown, Phil Rizzuto, and I did our own hit-and-run. We put it on. And that's highly unusual today. We did hit the ball. I'm not saying for a base hit, but we could make contact. I even put on the hit-and-run when Johnny Mize, a slow, burly guy, was on base. I had a special sign that the runner could pick up. It involved how many times I was tapping the bat on home plate and how I was holding it.

I don't think I used four bats a year. Now players use about 44. The bats are splintering, flying all over the place. It's not as good as the wood we had. Sometimes when you're the pitcher you've got to watch the bat flying at you more than the ball.

The way you'd lose the bat when I played was if the barrel would start to flake a little bit. I always had a thick-handled bat. Johnny Mize used one, too. DiMaggio used a thin handle. You might get more hits off the good part of the bat with a thick handle. You might get a little more carry.

The summer of 1949 would become a pressure-packed time with the Yankees fighting the Red Sox for the pennant. It was certainly a lot of pressure for a rookie like me. It's been written that I was battling ulcers that season. And maybe I was, but I didn't know it at the time. My stomach has always been my enemy. It was always very sensitive, but I didn't have bleeding ulcers or anything like that in '49. I might have had an ulcer that was growing. My serious ulcer hit after my service in Korea. Eventually, after I managed the Padres in 1980, I went into the hospital and had my stomach redone.

I was always a hyper guy, but I wasn't having any particular problems with stress or getting the food down in my rookie year. I always did eat light at breakfast before the game; almost all our home games were during the afternoons. I wasn't a hamburger guy, a ham and eggs guy. I'd eat Cream of Wheat and poached eggs and things like that before the game, but after that I was fine.

And it's been written that I was worried I might cost the Yankees the pennant with a fielding blunder or two. That's not true. I was in a new position, but second base suited me fine after playing mostly at third and short in the minors.

When I was forced out of the lineup, it wasn't because of nerves. I've had sinus problems all my life. Early in the '49 season I got a sinus infection and I was playing with a fever of 105 degrees. That was from wearing down, fatigue, and so forth, when your resistance gets low. I wasn't telling anybody, and finally I just had to give up and they took me out of the lineup.

I'm in pinstripes at age 17, but they belong to the 1942 Wellsville Yankees of the Pony League.

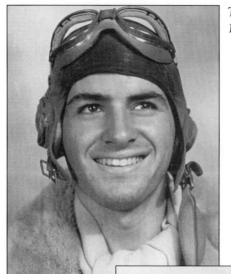

The making of a pilot in October 1942.

Getting ready for a flight in the navy's V-5 pilot training program at Alamosa, Colorado, in the winter of 1943.

With my mother, Pearl Coleman, while I was on leave from pilot training in July 1943.

In the Philippines with my fellow World War II pilots: (from left) Bud Madden, Bob Means, Art Mauer, and me.

I've made it to the 1947 Kansas City Blues of the American Association, a top Yankees farm team.

It's a Bay Area reunion with (from second to left) Bobby Brown, Frank Crosetti, and Charlie Silvera at the Yankees' 1948 spring training camp in St. Petersburg, Florida.

Proud to be a New York Yankee.

Eluding a slide by Jerry Scala of the Chicago White Sox and turning a double play at Comiskey Park in June 1950. PHOTO COURTESY OF AP/WIDE WORLD PHOTOS.

I'm receiving the Babe Ruth Award as Most Valuable Player of the 1950 World Series, presented by John Drebinger of The New York Times. PHOTO COURTESY OF AP/WIDE WORLD PHOTOS.

Captain Jerry Coleman, trying on a new Marine uniform in January 1952, a few months before going on active duty for the Korean War. PHOTO COURTESY OF AP/ WIDE WORLD PHOTOS.

Joe DiMaggio, newly retired, visits with me before ceremonies at Yankee Stadium on April 30, 1952, my last day in pinstripes before reporting to the Marine Corps. PHOTO COURTESY OF AP/WIDE WORLD PHOTOS.

I wanted to win that job so I subjected myself to some unpleasant treatments. They had this long needle that goes right through your bone to take the infected material out. The first one I had, I can still picture the doctor. He put this thing in my nose and then, boom, boom, he had an opening on the other end and they'd flush water through there. To this day I have sinus problems from time to time. But I never had anything like I had my first year in New York.

So I was out for a week or 10 days with that sinus problem and finally Casey Stengel asked me to pinch-hit against a left-handed pitcher in Chicago, and I got a triple. From that point on, he put me back in and I stayed.

Stengel, I would soon find out, was very impersonal. He was not a guy who put his arms around you. He wasn't a guy who went around and buddy-buddied with the players. In those days managers were much more aloof than they are today. He was not very much appreciated by the DiMaggios and the Rizzutos and the people who played for Joe McCarthy. McCarthy was a totally different animal, more attuned to the players' feelings. Stengel was egotistical in many ways.

He wasn't the kind of guy to give out compliments. He was a tough guy to play for. You'd go into the clubhouse and maybe you'd find that your name wasn't in the lineup. He never said anything. You just didn't play that day.

He had a lot to overcome. When he got the job, I saw a sign—"Yanks Hire Clown"—because Casey was a character and he had managed some bad ballclubs in the National League during the 1930s and '40s. He managed the Brooklyn Dodgers when they got the nickname "Dem Bums" and the Boston Braves.

But he was a brilliant, brilliant manger. He had the four qualities that I consider absolute musts in a manager.

He understood his players; he knew more about you in two weeks than you knew about yourself in 20 years. He knew about the social problems in baseball. He knew about when players had problems with other players.

He understood the fans; what they liked and what they needed and how to play up to them.

He understood the front office; what it wanted and how it handled things.

And—the single most important factor in New York—he understood the media. There were 10 papers in New York, the three wire services, and suburban papers, too. During road trips we had as many writers on a train as we had players. They were everywhere, although there weren't guys with a tape recorder floating around like today. So if you didn't understand the media in New York, you had a problem. That's why the Mets hired Stengel when they were getting started with a bunch of kids and guys over the hill. They needed somebody like that to take the brunt of what was going on with their bad ballclub. He was brilliant with the media. He would tell them, "Look, write what you want. Just don't hurt me."

And he's the only manager who I ever heard come in and say, "I blew it, that's mine. I blew it." I heard him say it three or four times. Apparently it was a change he made or didn't make with the pitchers. A mistake in his own mind. He'd say that to the players.

A lot of the players didn't like the way Stengel platooned them. Late in my career, when I was in and out of the lineup, we had an 11-game winning streak going. Then we lost a game, and I got benched. It ticked me off. Hank Bauer and Gene Woodling, a couple of pretty good outfielders, hated the platooning. So did Billy Johnson and Bobby Brown at third base. But Stengel knew which right-handed hitters couldn't hit some right-handed pitchers, and so on. He had a very, very brilliant baseball mind. Nobody was close to him.

I might have driven in 100 runs as a rookie if Stengel hadn't pinch-hit for me every time I turned around. I batted right-handed and, of course, he had left-handed bats in and out of the lineup—Tommy Henrich, Gene Woodling, Charlie Keller, Johnny Mize, and Cliff Mapes—and sometimes those guys were on the bench when I was due up. If it was a key situation, he would take me out and bring in one of the left-handed bats, which was obvious. I would do it myself.

I did have a pair of 4-for-4 days as a rookie against the same left-handed pitcher for the Philadelphia Athletics, Alex Kellner. The first time it happened was in April. I hit three singles off him in a game at Yankee Stadium, then hit a two-run homer into the lower left-field stands in the eighth inning to win the game 5-4. The man who shook my hand at home plate was George Stirnweiss, who was losing his job to me. He still couldn't play in the field because of that Opening-Day hand injury, but he was on base as a pinch-runner when I hit my home run. Kellner was the only guy I ever got four hits against in the same game. I don't remember what kind of pitches he threw, but he was pitching me wrong.

I hit a home run off another A's pitcher who was quite a courageous figure—a left-hander named Lou Brissie. He was wounded in December 1944 as an infantryman in the World War II campaign in Italy, and the doctors wanted to amputate his leg. But he had been signed by the A's out of Presbyterian College in South Carolina before the war and he hoped to pitch in the major leagues. He persuaded the doctors to try to save his leg, and they did, but he underwent more than 20 operations, and he pitched with a brace. He won 16 games in my rookie season and made the All-Star team.

Another Athletics pitcher in the late 1940s, Phil Marchildon, a right-hander from Ontario, had also survived a wartime ordeal. He joined the Royal Canadian Air Force after winning 17 games for the Athletics in 1942. He was a gunner on a Halifax bomber on his 26th mission in August 1944 when his plane was shot down off Nazi-occupied Denmark. He parachuted into the water and was picked up by a fisherman, who turned him over to the Germans, and he spent nine months as a prisoner of war. He was put through a forced march in the bitter winter of '45 before he was repatriated. They said he had barely recovered emotionally when he rejoined the A's.

The major league rosters still had many World War II veterans in that summer of '49, but I never spoke with opposing players about the war. You simply didn't talk to opponents back then. And the Yankees players didn't talk much about the war with each other. It was done. The memories would linger, but we didn't share them.

When I was breaking into the lineup, my father was still working for the post office in San Francisco. In fact, he worked with Bill McDougald, the father of Gil McDougald, who would become my teammate in the

Yankees infield during the 1950s. One day the Associated Press ran a photo of them sorting mail alongside each other.

As the '49 season moved along, I was becoming a fixture in the lineup, and I got some press notices back home beyond the wire-service accounts picked up by the newspapers. There was a profile of me and my family in June by a publication called *Incabus*, written for federal employees like my father. The headline said, "Fielding Sensation." Almost 60 years later, I still have it.

The story noted how my father, a postal worker, was "dispensing stamps at a local station" and it mentioned he had played in the minor leagues.

"You would expect parents with a son in the majors to be interested in his progress," the article said. "The Colemans are no exception. Daily they run through the sport pages with hawk-like vigilance. Local sheets are not sufficient. They also receive *The New York Times* and that Bible of Baseball, the *St. Louis Sporting News.* Jerry Sr. hops out of the apartment at midnight to buy a late paper and check up on the night games."

That story about our family wasn't quite complete. The readers didn't know what had happened at home when I was a youngster, what my father had done to my mother.

When I arrived in New York, the Yankees were the team that dominated sports. Baseball was *the* sport in the '40s and '50s. It dominated the sports pages and dominated the fans' interest. No one paid much attention to pro basketball, and the National Football League wasn't big either. When the New York Giants football team left the Polo Grounds and made Yankee Stadium their home field, they couldn't play there until the World Series was over. They would have three or four games on the road to open their season. The Yankees would not even let them on the field until baseball was through.

The Yankees were our religion—to be a Yankee to me was the greatest thing ever put on this earth. The impact of being a Yankee was so enormous as to be beyond belief. I never, ever heard about a player who didn't want to be a Yankee and I never, ever saw a Yankees player who wasn't upset if he was traded.

We used to take the train from Florida to New York, barnstorming through the South at the end of spring training, back when there were only eight American and eight National League teams. You'd wake up and look out the window, and at 6:00, 7:00 in the morning, there were people standing along the tracks and waving. How did they know we were coming? We were the Yankees—we were *it*.

But we never got arrogant about it. We never got conceited. The difference with the Yankees and other teams was, if you came in second with the Yankees, you lost. A lot of teams thought second place was pretty good. But with the Yankees, the pressure was absolutely intense. You had to win. The year we came in second to Cleveland, 1954, was Stengel's best year for winning—we won 103 games. But the point was, we lost.

In my rookie summer, I was living on Gerard Avenue, a block and a half from Yankee Stadium. On Saturday night (we played almost all our games during the day), you'd see dozens of mothers and their children in strollers. It was a very heavily Jewish area, middle class, working class. They were rolling their kids back and forth. It was wonderful; great people. You could go anyplace. We never thought about a problem at night. The whole feeling in the world was different then. The war was over, people were trying to recover, and everybody was doing the best they could. And then the George Washington Bridge double-decked and everyone went to the suburbs. But I can still think back and see all these mothers pushing their kids in strollers.

In those days we used to park on the curb outside Yankee Stadium. Trying to get to your car was a major challenge. DiMaggio would wait three or four hours after the game. They let him out the center-field fence with a cab waiting for him. He was so popular and so dominating that everybody wanted his autograph, and he couldn't do it.

They put the sawhorses out there to keep the crowds away, but the fans would go right through them. You got into your car, you couldn't sign anything, you couldn't write. That's when the besieged players would tell the kids, "Give me a postcard and I'll sign it and mail it back to you."

The players never asked to be paid for autographs—memorabilia and card shows were unheard of. The first time I saw someone sign for money was at the All-Star Game in San Francisco in 1961, when I was broadcasting it. Bob Feller was getting paid for his signature. It might have happened before, but it was the first time I saw it.

Ray Flynn, a former mayor of Boston, has told a delightful story about his quest for autographs when he was a youngster growing up in South Boston, and I'm a part of this tale. As he related it long afterward to the sportswriter Leigh Montville, he was shining shoes outside the Hotel Somerset. Ted Williams lived there and the Yankees were staying at the hotel for a series with the Red Sox. When the Yankees players came down to find taxis for the ride to Fenway Park, young Ray got a piece of paper and an old pen and asked us for autographs. But his pen didn't work.

As he told it, "Jerry Coleman reaches into his suit jacket and takes out a gold pen. He signs and hands the pen to someone else and someone else, and now Joe DiMaggio is there. For some reason, he thinks I'm Jerry Coleman's nephew or something, and he smiles and takes the gold pen and signs.

"While he's signing, Ted Williams comes down. He comes over to Joe and me. He takes the gold pen and signs. They're talking, Ted Williams and Joe DiMaggio, how are ya, back and forth, and for some reason Williams thinks that I'm DiMaggio's nephew or something. He says, 'Hey, it's getting late. Let's get to the ballpark.' We get into the cab, Ted Williams, Joe DiMaggio, and me...

"I have Joe DiMaggio on one side of me. I have Ted Williams on the other side. I have both of their autographs. And I also have Jerry Coleman's gold pen in my pocket. Who ever has made out better than this?"

Ray Flynn mentioned that my gold pen was in my suit jacket. We had a dress code on the Yankees—a jacket, shirt, and tie. During the mid- or late '50s, they gave us sport jackets with an "NY" on the pocket where the handkerchief went, though that didn't last too long. I never thought that dressing formally on road trips was an imposition. DiMaggio, in fact, showed up at Yankee Stadium in a suit and tie as well.

We traveled by train and we stayed together more than players do today. On trains, we were always together. Now players get on a plane, hunker up to a computer or watch a movie, some play cards. Then you get off and go your separate ways.

In my early years with the Yankees, we had upper and lower berths. The regulars were in the lower berths and the reserves were in the upper berths. And then at the end of my Yankees career we all had our separate compartments; close the door and lock out the world. We had two cars of players and writers, and a diner car, always at the end of a train. We never saw the other passengers. No one came through those three Yankees cars. We'd go to our diner car and have our dinner, which was always a steak if you wanted it. Then you'd hang around in the diner and play cards if you wanted, or you'd go to your little room and read, and wake up in the next town.

I never had any trouble sleeping on those trains. Some people did. We had a trainer named Gus Mauch. He'd go up and down the train calling out "Nembutal, Seconal"—they were sleeping pills. One was yellow, one was red. In 1950, when he was the MVP, Rizzuto took one every night on the train. Once, I think we had a trip that went from Cleveland to Detroit to Chicago. I took one on the way to Detroit but I slept much too late. I couldn't take those things. I had a terrible time with them. I'd never wake up.

In the off-season, ballplayers went to work like everyone else. When we weren't playing, we had everyday jobs to help pay the rent. I had worked for that slaughterhouse. I worked for a company that tore buildings down. I worked in a tire factory—I came out looking like a piece of coal when the day was over. I worked on the Embarcadero in San Francisco, lugging stuff around. I worked at the Libby's company, hauling boxes and crates of canned fruit. I drove through blizzards in upstate New York. They'd offer you $200 or $300 to go up there and make a speech, and that was a lot of money then. Coming back from up around Binghamton, I would be on these two-lane highways with trucks coming over the top of the hill, lights looking at you, and you're coming down, and it's snowing. Every time I went up there, it seemed there was a blizzard on the way back. I look at it now, I must have been insane. I should have stayed in the town where I was until it stopped snowing.

I needed a job during the winter all through my baseball career. I didn't care what it was as long as it was legal and they paid me. I had a wife and children to support.

As spring 1949 turned to summer, I was hoping to double my salary before too long. When I signed a Yankees contract during spring training, it was for $5,000. When I survived the cutdown date, which was June 15, it jumped to $7,000 for the year. But a World Series check might come close to doubling that. Considering the history of the Yankees, it seemed a reasonable expectation. But the Boston Red Sox had their own ideas.

The Great Pennant Race

"The Yankees were *the* team at the time, and I was proud to be a part of it. We didn't think about the attention given to DiMaggio and, soon, to Mickey Mantle. We just wanted to win."

7

The Great Pennant Race

When you talk about the pennant race of '49, you have to start with Joe DiMaggio and his remarkable comeback.

We were barnstorming in Texas during spring training, and DiMaggio disappeared from the ballclub. His heel spur problems had acted up again, so he went back to New York and he was out for the first two months.

It was now late June, and we were playing a three-game series in Fenway Park. We had a four-and-a-half-game lead over the Athletics and a five-game lead over the Red Sox and Tigers—our pitching gave us a red-hot start. DiMaggio finally came back. He hit four home runs, drove in nine runs, and led us to three wins. We swept the Red Sox. Now we were eight games ahead of them. Joe was the guy, and it was one of baseball's great unknown feats.

I played with Joe in the last three years of his career, when he was tailing off. He was never the same player after World War II. But as for his first six or seven years in baseball, as far as numbers go, nobody was even close to him. In 1941, when Joe and Ted Williams were the dominant players—Williams hitting .406, DiMaggio with his 56-game hitting streak—Joe struck out 13 times. We have guys do that in a week today. You don't think anything of it. I hate strikeouts because when you strike out, nothing happens. Joe always hit the ball.

Along with Willie Mays, Joe was maybe the greatest player overall you could want to see—he could run, he could field, he could throw, his batting average was way up there, and he hit for power, though his home-run totals were cut down by playing in Yankee Stadium. You had to hit the ball 450 feet to get out of the ballpark unless you hit it right down the line in left field.

His senses on the field were unbelievable. Only once did I see him make a mistake. He caught a ball, started jogging, and realized it was the second out, not the third out, and did he get rid of that in a hurry. He was perfect. Mickey Mantle had more power and more speed, but he struck out 1,700 times, for heaven's sake. DiMaggio struck out 369 times in his whole career.

DiMaggio and Mantle were totally different people. Joe knew exactly who he was, what he was, what he represented, and the team he represented. He was the man in sports. Joe Louis, Joe DiMaggio, Don Budge—they were the dominant factors the way Tiger Woods is in golf today.

Joe always showed up in a shirt, tie, and jacket. He understood life. I don't think he got past the 10th grade in high school, but he was a very intelligent person.

Mickey was a kid. He never understood how big he was. He was the biggest superstar after Williams and DiMaggio, and he never understood the dominance. When we went to spring training, we'd go to Miami for a week. If DiMaggio went out to a nightclub, he'd get a place in a corner, the dark recesses, and no one knew he was there. Mickey, they put him up in front of the stage, and he'd stand up and take a bow.

DiMaggio and Mantle were both good men, but the differences between them were enormous. Mantle was a wonderful man, but he was also shy and naïve. His frustrations mounted over the years. Most of his drinking problems didn't surface during his playing career. I roomed with him for two seasons, and I can vouch for that. His problems came after he retired—when the bright lights had dimmed and there was nothing for him. That's when it got tough for Mickey.

But I don't think that DiMaggio was very happy. I didn't think he really enjoyed his celebrity. His first wife, Dorothy Arnold, was an actress; I don't know what happened there, but there was a split. Of course, he married the one woman he should never have married. Joe was a guy from the old school—women should be at home, taking care of the house, the family—and he married the most glamorous woman in the world. It was the opposite of everything that he thought he wanted. But he loved Marilyn Monroe—he really loved her. If you wanted to lose DiMaggio, you'd say, "Hey, how's Marilyn doing, Joe?" That would be the last time he'd talk to you. He cut a lot of people off.

Joe seldom showed emotion. One day after striking out, he came into the dugout and kicked a bag full of balls. We all went "ooh." Doing that must have really hurt. He sat down with the sweat popping out on his forehead and clenched his fists without ever saying a word.

I thoroughly enjoyed my time with him. I spent two months with him during the Vietnam War on a tour with baseball people just before the Tet offensive. I spent many trips with him, and we got together at dinners.

He was always in the public eye, everyone wanting his autograph, and that was hard for him. In 1950 we were going to spring training. We got on a plane in San Francisco, went to L.A., Fort Worth, New Orleans, and then to Tampa and St. Petersburg. In Fort Worth he said, "Let's get a paper." We had a half hour to get the paper and come back for the next leg of our flight. I told him, "Okay." We were walking down this long corridor. This was before television, when every ballplayer would come into people's living rooms, so to speak. But I never saw so many people come to attention in my life. Everybody in that airport knew who Joe was.

After baseball, when I was doing promotions for the Van Heusen clothing company, I used Joe in several spots in New York and San Francisco. I'd see him a lot.

When I began broadcasting on the West Coast, I got a renewed sense of the problems that he had in public. One time he said, "Hey, take me to the airport." It was the Orange County airport that they call John Wayne Airport now. So we hopped in the car and off we went. When we got there, he said, "You got to come in with me." He could never be alone. He had to have someone buffering him. I didn't realize it at the time, but that was his life. It was a lousy life from my standpoint. I think he adored the attention he got but didn't like the part where he had to give back.

A lot of the big stars love the adulation, they love getting their picture in the paper and in the news. But it can be a difficult time, especially for a guy in the limelight of the country. It was especially tough for Mantle, coming from Commerce, Oklahoma. How do you do that? I had a little bit of it, but nothing like DiMaggio or Mantle had.

DiMaggio appeared at a lot of Old-Timers' Day events at Yankee Stadium when I was broadcasting Yankees games. His one rule was that he had to be the last guy introduced. Once they had a promotional event for an all-time baseball team. I think it was in Boston, and Williams and DiMaggio were on the same team. They were voted in along with Musial and all these other superstars. So how do you introduce DiMaggio and Williams? They solved the problem by bringing them in from opposite sides at the same time.

Somebody told a story about the night that Joe DiMaggio was in the first President Bush's box at a game somewhere, and they handed Joe a dozen balls to sign. Every place he went, something happened. It was incredible.

I don't do many autograph sessions. I did one in New York some time back. They said, "We got you signing, and also Rizzuto." But DiMaggio was the big attraction. I said, "You don't need Phil and me." DiMaggio's line was a block long and ours was 50 feet. A signed picture by DiMaggio was around $150 or $170, and a ball was $150. Joe signed and signed and signed and signed. My understanding is that Mantle made more than $1 million a year signing autographs on balls and whatnot.

I had a friend who asked me once if I would get DiMaggio's autograph. I said, "God Almighty, they sell these things for $150, $175." But Joe was very gracious. He signed three balls and three pictures and gave them to me. That, to me, is one of the greatest honors I ever had in my life. He once refused to sign a bat for Whitey Ford, but I don't know why.

∞ • ∞

As for the pennant race in '49, Stengel did a lot of platooning while DiMaggio was out for the first half of the season. Tommy Henrich split time between first base and the outfield. Tommy was a little testy—he wasn't Mr. Charm, but he was a great clutch hitter, and Old Reliable was a perfect description for him. In '49 Henrich was there all year to keep us going. He was really the star of that season. He led us in home runs with 24, and outside of DiMaggio's hitting .346 over the second half of the season, Henrich was our leading batter, even though he hit only .287. We weren't in the mold of the power-hitting Yankees teams of old that summer.

Charlie Keller, an outstanding outfielder for the Yankees in his day, was at the end of his career when I got there. He had a ruptured disk that left him rigid in the back. Hank Bauer and Gene Woodling, who would become fixtures during all those pennant-winning seasons of the 1950s, saw a lot of outfield action in '49, and so did Cliff Mapes and Johnny Lindell.

With Phil and me in the middle, Bobby Brown at third base, backed up by Billy Johnson, and Henrich at first base much of the time, we had a solid infield.

What really did it for us was our great four-man pitching staff and our great defense. We had Vic Raschi, Allie Reynolds, Eddie Lopat, and Tommy Byrne starting, and as our reliever we had Joe Page, who most fans don't know anything about today but might have been as good as any relief pitcher in history for a couple of years.

The Red Sox had a stronger hitting lineup—Ted Williams, Dom DiMaggio, and Al Zarilla in the outfield, and Billy Goodman, Bobby Doerr, Junior Stephens, and Johnny Pesky in the infield, with Birdie Tebbetts catching.

Williams was on his way toward an MVP season in 1949—a .343 batting average, 43 home runs, and 159 runs batted in. Doerr, Pesky, and Dom DiMaggio hit over .300, and Stephens and Goodman were close to it. Stephens was a tremendous power hitter, although he was not a good shortstop. Of course, Williams was the greatest hitter of his generation, maybe the greatest ever.

The big pitchers for the Red Sox were Mel Parnell, an outstanding lefty, and Ellis Kinder, though he had a reputation as a drinker. They won 48 games between them that year. And Joe McCarthy, who had won all those pennants with the Yankees in the 1930s and early '40s, was managing them, still a figure of affection for the veteran Yankees like DiMaggio, Henrich, and Rizzuto.

With DiMaggio back in the lineup by midsummer, we figured we had this pennant race won. But the Red Sox went on a tear, and going into the final weekend, they were ahead of us by one game. We were playing them twice at Yankee Stadium and we had to win both games to take the pennant.

We had Allie Reynolds—the Super Chief—pitching on Saturday. But he was rocked and he did everything wrong. Finally in the third inning—with the bases loaded and two runs in—Stengel took him out and brought in Joe Page.

Everybody else might have been worried, but not Joe. He ended up walking the next two batters, though, to make it 4-0, and I was thinking, *Oh, good lord, there goes my World Series check.* I really felt we were done.

In the bottom of the third, Rizzuto was at bat with Birdie Tebbetts behind the plate. At that time, teams had these kids called "bonus babies" whom they had to keep on the roster because they signed them for a lot of money. It was a way to discourage teams from paying too much for untried kids. Tebbetts teased Rizzuto, saying, "I guess we'll pitch so-and-so tomorrow"—meaning the "bonus baby." It was a guy named Frank Quinn, who had been signed out of Yale and had pitched in only a few games. Tebbetts was telling us that the Red Sox had the game won and the pennant clinched, so the next day's game wouldn't mean anything.

But Page, our star closer, went six-plus innings and shut them down; they never got another run.

Relief pitching was just starting to become a specialty. Back then, when you weren't a starter, you went to the bullpen and they might call on you next month. Now they rotate them pretty evenly and they have bullpens that are much stronger than ever before. Now they don't have just one guy. The thought process of playing the game is totally different.

So Page played an unusual role for his day, and he was in his glory, but the '47 and '49 seasons were his only terrific years. He was an alcoholic, and I guess it caught up with him. He was the only Yankees teammate I remember who really had a drinking problem. A lot of my teammates did some heavy drinking and got away with it. But Berra never drank, Rizzuto never drank, Bobby Brown didn't drink, I didn't. There were more who didn't drink than did—by light-years. DiMaggio would have a glass of wine but never drank seriously. Mantle, yes, he had a problem, but it was mostly after he left baseball. Billy Martin also would drink.

Page was the victim of a practical joke one day when he was evidently hung over. Eddie Lopat was a tough competitor on the mound, but he also liked to spring jokes. Eddie and Joe Page and a couple of other Yankees went fishing in Florida, and Joe went into their cabin to sleep it off. They hung a big silver bucket on his line. "Hey, Joe, you got a fish," they told him. So he came out, and he was tugging away at this thing. Finally he said, "Man, look at the mouth on that thing." He saw this huge opening—it was the bucket. They were howling.

But on that final Saturday in '49, Page was the best. While he was shutting the Red Sox down, we pecked away and pecked away, and Johnny Lindell hit a home run in the eighth inning to give us a 5-4 lead. That's how the game ended. It was our greatest comeback when we needed it most. So now we were tied for first place going into Sunday.

Vic Raschi was pitching for us, and we were leading 1-0 when Henrich hit a homer leading off the eighth. After that, we loaded the bases with two out, and I came to the plate. Some of the fans might have figured that Stengel would pinch-hit for me. I don't know if Johnny Mize was available. We got Mize from the New York Giants late in the year, and in Chicago he dove for a ball and jammed his shoulder. That hadn't been a good day for us. That same afternoon, Henrich had backed into the Comiskey Park wall and he was out for a while. But we had that two-run lead when I was due up, and Casey wanted me to stay in for defense, I guess. If we had a one-run lead or were even, I might not have hit.

Ellis Kinder had started for the Red Sox, but Ted Hughson, a big right-hander who had been a 20-game winner twice, was pitching in relief. He threw one high and tight. I got my bat out before the ball could hit me on the head. I hit it on the trademark, a looping drive over the head of Bobby Doerr, playing second base, and in front of Al Zarilla, the right fielder. Three runs scored, and I was thrown out at third base trying for a triple. It was not what I would call a fierce line drive, but it was effective. At that time, nobody thought that it meant anything. My double made it 5-0. We figured it was over.

But the Red Sox had two men on in the top of the ninth and then Doerr hit a ball that DiMaggio couldn't catch up with. He had been out with pneumonia and didn't have his strength back. Joe retrieved the ball, got it back in, and just ran off the field into the dugout. He thought he should have caught that ball and he felt he was hurting the team. Stengel moved Cliff Mapes from right field to center, shifted Hank Bauer from left field to right, and put Gene Woodling into left field. I'll give Joe credit for that. A lot of guys wouldn't have the sense or the dignity to protect the club that way.

So then it was 5-2 following Doerr's triple. Billy Goodman singled in a run with two out, and Birdie Tebbetts came to bat. Henrich, who was playing first base, came over to talk to Raschi. Vic said, "Gimme the goddamned ball." Henrich never said a word. He did a 360 and went back to first base. In those days, complete games were the norm. Now managers don't even wait. You blink in the sixth inning and they bring in somebody from the bullpen.

Raschi got Tebbetts to hit a foul pop off the first-base line. I went over to catch the ball, but Henrich had gone over as well, and Tommy said, "I got it."

I'm just a rookie, and he's the guy Mel Allen called Old Reliable. So I'm thinking, "Yes, sir." Henrich caught the ball, and we won the pennant. That remains my greatest thrill in baseball.

Today they parade around the field and shake hands and jump on each other and wave bats when they celebrate. But we just ran into the clubhouse and had our chaotic festivities inside.

The Yankees were *the* team at that time, and I was proud to be a part of it. We didn't think about the attention given to DiMaggio and, soon, to Mickey Mantle. We just wanted to win. Being a Yankee was the ultimate goal in life at the time. There were a lot of teams that were great in that era. The Brooklyn Dodgers might have had a better team than we had at times. The Red Sox might have had a better ballclub some summers, at least on paper, but we had the great pitching and we had defense and that image of never wanting to lose—period.

A little later in my career, we lost a game to the Chicago White Sox 15-0. It was like someone had shot us. Losing 1-0, 2-1, 5-3, that's one thing. Losing 15-0, I'll never forget it. It's still in my mind a half century later. That's how much we wanted to win and how badly we took losing—especially losing badly.

But now we had won the pennant again after being beaten out by the Indians and the Red Sox in 1948.

We faced the Brooklyn Dodgers in the World Series for the second time in three years. I was with the Kansas City farm team in 1947, but who can forget the '47 Series? Floyd Bevens, a Yankees pitcher of no great renown, lost what would have been the first no-hitter in World Series history in Game 4 when Cookie Lavagetto hit a two-run, two-out double off the scoreboard at Ebbets Field in the ninth inning for a 3-2 Dodgers victory. And Al Gionfriddo, the little Dodgers outfielder hardly anyone had heard of, made that great catch off DiMaggio in front of the Yankees bullpen at the Stadium in Game 6. Joe kicked the dirt in frustration approaching second base, one of the only times he would display emotion on the ballfield. But the Yankees still won the Series in seven games.

We opened the '49 World Series at Yankee Stadium, with Reynolds facing Don Newcombe, who was a great, great pitcher, and the first outstanding African American pitcher in the major leagues. Nobody had better stuff. The first time I saw Newcombe, he was pitching for Montreal in 1948 when I was with Newark. We had a leadoff batter named Jay Defani, and I was hitting second. We had heard about how hard Newcombe could throw. His second pitch hit Defani in the head. After that, we lost all interest in doing something off Newk.

The old Yankee Stadium held 70,000 or so. Well, there was nothing more daunting than hitting a fastball pitcher like Newcombe on a warm, sunny October afternoon at the Stadium with all those white shirts in the background out in center field. Raschi had the benefit of that and so did Reynolds. They were both power pitchers. Lopat was a stuff pitcher—they called him the Junkman. He wasn't a guy who really blew you away.

Newcombe and Reynolds were locked in a scoreless game through eight innings in the Series opener. Then Henrich hit a homer in the ninth, and we won it 1–0. But we lost the next day 1–0 with Preacher Roe, a tough cookie, beating Raschi. We went on to win the next three games, behind Byrne, Lopat, and Raschi. In contrast to '47, this wasn't the most exciting World Series—it was almost an anticlimax for Yankees fans after our thrilling pennant race with the Red Sox—but it was plenty satisfying for me.

I had a good Series with three doubles and four runs batted in. Bobby Brown hit .500 (6-for-12) and drove in five runs. We scored 21 runs in those five games, with Bobby and me accounting for nine of them. DiMaggio was 2-for-18, but he did drive in a couple of runs.

My wife, Louise, and my sister, Rosemarie, were at all the World Series games. They were sitting behind first base for the opener at the Stadium. My sister remembers that when the ball flew off Henrich's bat on his game-winning homer, Joe Cronin, the former Red Sox shortstop and manager, a Bay Area guy, got up from his seat even before the ball went over the fence. "That's it," Cronin said.

When we had our World Series meetings before all those October games against the Dodgers in the decade following the war, the guys who we really centered on were Jackie Robinson and Pee Wee Reese. You go through every player—Gil Hodges, Billy Cox, Roy Campanella,

Carl Furillo, Duke Snider, Andy Pafko. But Robinson and Reese were the ones who could beat you. Reese could bunt, he could hit-and-run, he had a little bit of power.

When Robinson got on base, he'd drive you crazy. Billy Martin was playing second base, and I was playing shortstop in one of the World Series games in the '50s. I had watched Robinson and the way he'd dash around second base and get midway between second and third. You threw the ball to second, he'd go to third. You threw it to third, he'd go to second. A great base runner. I saw him dash around, and Billy got the ball. I said, "I got him." I sneaked in behind Jackie and I yelled, "Billy." He threw the ball into left field. I was going to kill him. The one chance to get Robinson between second and third, and we blew it.

Martin Luther King Jr. gets much of the credit in the civil rights movement, but Robinson started it. He's the guy who really broke down the doors first. I'm not just talking sports. I'm talking all over the country.

In October 1972 I saw Jackie in Cincinnati at the World Series. He was being honored on the 25th anniversary of his breaking the major league color barrier. I went over to say hello: "Hi, Jack." But he didn't respond. I said, "Jerry Coleman."

He said, "Oh, hi, hi."

He was nearly blind. That was such a tragic thing when you think what he once was and what he was then. Two weeks later, he was dead of a heart attack at 53.

I'll conclude remembering Jackie on a lighter note.

We wore the same number. Howard Cosell, a good friend of mine, had a running gag any time he would introduce me at a function. "Gerald Francis Coleman, No. 42," Howard would say. "The wrong 42."

That summer of '49 was a terrific time for me, especially considering that I came to spring training dubious I would even make the team.

I hit .275 and I led American League second basemen in fielding. The Associated Press named me the league's Rookie of the Year. (The baseball writers gave their rookie award to Roy Sievers, the St. Louis Browns' outfielder.)

I got a check for $5,400 as a winning share for the World Series, not far from my regular-season pay of $7,000.

As for that blooper that became a three-run double in the regular season's final game, I brooded a little over the fact that it wasn't a solid hit. But one time I was with Joe McCarthy at a banquet, and he very simply said, "Well, you didn't strike out." I thought, *I didn't hit the ball well but I hit it in a very opportune spot in right field.*

I teased Ted Williams about that hit once. He replied, "You lucky son of a gun. It's the worst hit I ever saw in my entire life." And I joked, "Ted, let me tell you about that. Now you're out in left field. It's bright and sunny. You can't even see. It's all dark in the infield. When I hit it, you saw the cover of the ball drop to the ground. The core is still in orbit."

Of course, for the Red Sox it was indeed the worst hit. It cost them the pennant. I joked about this with Ted just that one time. I realized it touched him. He and I got along quite well over the years, but he didn't appreciate being kidded about that.

Ted had a bad rap in Boston because he was *the* guy, and if he didn't do it in the way the sportswriters wanted him to do it, they took after him. There was a sportswriter named Dave Egan—they called him the Colonel—who was a hatchet man.

Ted was a delightful person and generous as hell, but it never came out that way because the press just nailed him all the time. It's well remembered how once, when he hit a home run, he jumped in the air and spit at the press box. It was a game against the Yankees. And he never doffed his cap—even that afternoon at Fenway Park when he hit the last home run of his career in the final game he played there. That was Ted, but he was a great guy.

Ted was a San Diego native and he used to make the Padres' banquets. John Moores, the Padres' owner, was able to get him in his later years. One time Ted was at the home of Larry Lucchino, a Padres executive then, and Tony Gwynn was among the people there. Ted was happy to share his incomparable knowledge of hitting. He got ahold of Tony. He didn't tell him how to hold his bat or give him advice on his stance. He told him about the "thought" of hitting—the mental process. Ted insisted that you have to know what to look for, understand the pitcher, how he's doing it, and be ready for him. "Gotta be ready, gotta be ready," was how he put it.

Gwynn led the league in hitting four consecutive times late in his career—all after the Williams conferences. When Ted managed the second version of the Washington Senators, he improved the batting averages of many of the guys greatly from the year before, just emphasizing the thought process in hitting. The Senators had a team batting average of .224 in 1968, the year before Ted became their manager. In Ted's first season managing them, the overall batting average jumped to .251. People think that hitting is just stance and grip and reactions. It's the mental process that really makes great hitters.

The last time I saw Ted, they had brought him out to a hospital in San Diego for treatment, and I went to visit him. You needed two 200-pounders to carry this man in, put him in a bed, and sit him up. He couldn't really speak. I thought to myself, *Why are they keeping this man alive?* Then they took him back to Florida, where he died.

Returning to that summer of 1949, they had a parade on Market Street in San Francisco after we won the World Series, honoring DiMaggio, myself, and Charlie Silvera, the backup catcher who grew up with me in the Bay Area.

That winter, after working in manual-labor jobs during the off-season, I got myself a white-collar job—literally. I became more sophisticated. I was a haberdashery salesman in San Francisco at a store called Hastings. I didn't make a lot of money on commission because anything that was good, I gave away. I felt guilty. Here I've got this check for the World Series victory and I'm selling things while my fellow salesmen were busting their chops just to make a living. When someone came in, the supervisor would say, "Mr. Coleman, would you handle so-and-so?" Sometimes the customer would buy a tie, but sometimes he would buy two suits and spend $200 or $300. If that happened, I'd give that sale to one of the people on the floor who wasn't as lucky as I was. I'd say to the supervisor, "Mr. Jones, please write this up and give him the sale," because they were on commission.

The Yankees won the World Series every year from 1949 to 1953. I was one of 12 Yankees to play on all those teams, though I missed most of '52 and '53 when I was called back into the Marines for the Korean War. As we went through the streak of five in a row, the enthusiasm lessened. It wasn't nearly as much fun as it was the first time. But we did have Sophie Tucker, Ray Bolger, Bob Hope, and all the Broadway stars at our victory parties at the Waldorf or the Vanderbilt. Every major star that was in range was there. It was like a Hollywood premiere.

For that first World Series championship, I was grateful to have the $5,400 winners' check. Of course, the Yankees got $320,000 a man for winning the 1998 World Series. Now *that's* money.

The Making of a Dynasty

"I thought, *If you need me, I'm here*. I've always been that way. I've always felt that your country is more important than anything you do in your private life."

8

The Making of a Dynasty

The 1950 season was probably my best year with the Yankees, though nothing would beat that thrill of edging out the Red Sox and winning a pennant for the first time. I played all but one game that year and hit .287, my highest average ever. I hit six home runs and drove in 69 runs. Those weren't exactly DiMaggio numbers, but I would never match those totals again. And Rizzuto and I were teaming once more for smooth middle-infield play.

But halfway through the season came the news that stunned an America only recently emerged from World War II. Just like Pearl Harbor Day, it was a Sunday morning (Saturday night in Washington). On June 25 thousands of North Korean troops crossed the 38th parallel, dividing the two Koreas, and began a rout of our South Korean allies.

The Yankees split a Sunday doubleheader with the Tigers in Detroit, but I doubt that anyone was paying much attention beyond the ballpark. President Truman rushed back to Washington from a trip to his hometown of Independence, Missouri, and pledged to push back the Communists. Fighting under a United Nations resolution, America would be at war again, not even five full years after V-J Day.

The nation's armed forces had been cut severely since the end of World War II, and the Marines were no exception. In fact, the Corps was fortunate to have fended off a proposal that the air force absorb its aviation units. But the Marines quickly went into action. Two weeks after the North Koreans invaded the south, the 1st Provisional Marine Brigade, consisting of 6,500 ground troops and aviation personnel, was activated at Camp Pendleton, California. It sailed for Korea from San Diego in mid-July.

Marines began coming ashore on August 2 to protect the southern port of Pusan, the South Korean capital of Seoul having already fallen. The next day Marine pilots flying gull-winged Corsair fighters raided North Korean installations, taking off from the escort carrier *Sicily*. They were soon joined by Corsairs flying off the escort carrier *Baedong Strait*.

On September 15 the 1st Marine Division led the first major coun-terattack by United Nations forces with a surprise amphibious assault at the North Korean–occupied port of Inchon. Two weeks later the Marines had wrested Seoul from Communist control.

What did all this mean to me personally? When the Korean War broke out, the Marines realized, "Wow, we don't have any pilots." At least not enough. I was on the reserve list. When officers got out of the service after World War II, they were put on an inactive status, so they didn't really get out. That's what happened to me. The draft was on, but you can't draft a pilot—and it takes a year and a half to train one. I had no thought of being called up. This was Korea, a little peninsula. It was a "police action," it was "over there." It was 10,000 miles away. The war in Korea wasn't something I gave much thought to, so far as my personal situation went.

I had enough to be excited about, what with the prospect of another pennant victory and, before that, my first appearance at an All-Star Game, in Chicago's Comiskey Park. Bobby Doerr of the Red Sox started at second base, but I came in for him. I had one chance and booted it, and I got up twice and struck out. (It was a worse day for Ted Williams, who hit the wall making a catch in the first inning and learned later he had broken his elbow.)

But I was there, and it turned out to be one of the more exciting All-Star Games and the first one to go into extra innings. The St. Louis Cardinals' second baseman, Red Schoendienst, won it for the National League, 4–3, with a home run in the fourteenth inning.

Back then there were none of the trappings you have today, like the home-run derby and all those parties. When he owned the Padres, Ray

Kroc was the guy who started all that hype. He opened the San Diego ballpark for the workout the day before they had the All-Star Game there in 1978, and 30,000 people came. Dave Winfield threw a cookie-and-doughnuts party for 10,000 youngsters at a hotel hall in San Diego. A half-dozen players from both teams joined him in talking to the kids. Baseball realized it had something more than the game itself. Back in 1950 I took an overnight train from New York to Chicago, played the game, and that night I took another train home. That was it. Nobody paid any attention otherwise—the All-Star Game was it.

After all those years where the game was simply an exhibition—a chance to see baseball's best—now they've tagged on this thing where the league that wins the All-Star Game gains the home-field advantage for its pennant-winner in the World Series. I don't agree with that. The home-field edge should alternate between leagues the way it had been. Home field is a big deal. It's insignificant as to which team wins the All-Star Game. Nobody cares. But it is a showpiece for baseball, and there should be a penalty for any player who opts out for reasons other than injury. It's important to bring your best out there. You want to see the superstars compete.

In that 1950 season the Yankees still had great pitching with Raschi, Reynolds, Lopat, and Byrne, but we got even stronger when we brought up a young left-hander from our Kansas City farm club—Whitey Ford. He went 9-0, then finally lost a game while pitching in relief. He was facing the Athletics' Sam Chapman, a right-handed-batting outfielder with good power and, incidentally, a former All-American football player at California. Chapman hit one over the left-field wall in the ninth inning at Philadelphia's Shibe Park for a game-winning two-run homer. But Ford was just brilliant that year.

We beat out the Detroit Tigers by three games for the pennant, and this time we faced the Philadelphia Phillies in the World Series—the team known as the Whiz Kids because they had so many young players. They had good pitching with Jim Konstanty, Robin Roberts, and Curt Simmons, and a lineup including Richie Ashburn and Del Ennis in the outfield.

It was a low-scoring Series, but I got some timely hits. In Game 1 at Shibe Park, my fly ball in the fourth inning drove in Bobby Brown, who had doubled, for a 1-0 win over Konstanty. The next day I scored a run and then DiMaggio gave us a 2-1 victory with a tenth-inning home run.

When the Series arrived at Yankee Stadium, I came to the plate in the ninth inning with the game tied, 2-2, two men on and two out. I already had two of the Yankees' six hits that day and I scored the second run.

In his "Views of Sport" column in the *New York Herald Tribune* the next day, Red Smith described the scene:

> Now he was up again but most of the 64,505 witnesses weren't looking. Most of them were watching Russ Meyer, a somewhat flamboyant Philadelphia pitcher who bears watching because he does interesting things, like getting his nose bitten in saloons.
>
> "He never loses his swagger," a Philadelphia newspaperman was saying of Meyer. "He lost nine games in a row this summer and he never lost that strut."
>
> "He may lose it in a second," a guy said.
>
> In a second, Coleman had his third hit.
>
> It was a long fly to left center which the Philadelphia outfielders chased hopelessly for a little while and then gave up. Coleman ran to first base and Gene Woodling ran home with the winning run, and Meyer dropped like an old, ungartered sock.
>
> Across the infield, Coleman was trotting toward the Yankee bench, and Bill Dickey, who had been coaching at first, trotted behind him whacking him where he sits. The Yankees were one game away from their 13th world championship.

I was self-effacing after the game in describing the hit for the sportswriters.

The Associated Press quoted me as saying, "I thought the team was going to win, but I didn't think I'd be that instrumental in the victory."

The Associated Press's Ted Smits wrote, "Yes, that's the way he talks, smiling all the time and looking more as if he belonged on a college team than on the Yankees."

As for my single, I described it this way: "Actually, I think it was a ball that should have been caught. Richie Ashburn was playing me in right-center and it looked as if Jack Mayo in left field was too close to the foul line. The ball went right between them."

Stengel wasn't all that exuberant, considering that we had won three times and were on the brink of a sweep. Casey dwelled on the fact we had played three low-scoring games. As he put it, "Their pitchers are awful good or else we're in a terrible slump."

Whitey Ford was pitching in Game 4 at the Stadium. He had a 5-0 shutout with two down in the ninth, but Woodling dropped a fly ball to left. It was sunny and bright in left field and hard to pick up the ball. Stengel wanted Ford to get a shutout, but Woodling's muff brought in two runs. Stengel took Ford out, bringing Allie Reynolds in. This is where Woodling and Stengel ended up as mortal enemies forever. Stengel ran on top of the dugout steps and waved back, back to Woodling, thinking he was playing too shallow. It showed Gene up very badly, and Gene never forgave Stengel for that. Both of them are probably arguing about it in heaven someplace. We won the game anyway, 5-2, for a sweep and our second straight World Series championship.

I was given the Babe Ruth plaque as the Most Valuable Player of the World Series. We scored only 11 runs, but I had knocked in three of them, twice producing the game-winner.

My mother came to the World Series from San Francisco with her sister, Marie. She had never been out of California before. It would be the only time she saw me play professionally, except for an exhibition game we once had in Phoenix. She wasn't an emotional-type person but I know she had a great time. I was concentrating on the games so much that I wasn't thinking a lot about how she felt, but she was thrilled to death because I had a good Series.

As Christmas 1950 grew nearer, it seemed that the North Koreans would be beaten back. Then came the epic battle of the Chosin Reservoir, when thousands of Chinese Communist troops entered the war from Manchuria, charging down from the mountains in an attempt to wipe out the 1st Marine Division. After fierce fighting in snow and brutal cold, the Marines carried out a successful withdrawal through nearly 80 miles of mountain road.

The Korean War was showing no signs of ending by spring 1951, but I hadn't heard from the Marine Corps and I was back at second base for my third season as a Yankee. This was Mickey Mantle's rookie year and Joe DiMaggio's last season.

My first impression of Mantle was that he could run like hell but struck out too much. And as great as he would become, he was never the skilled outfielder that DiMaggio was.

As for a relationship between Mantle and DiMaggio in that summer of '51, it was probably stark terror for Mickey and "Who is this upstart?" for Joe. DiMaggio didn't let much bother him or let you know much about how he thought. He wasn't one who said, "Hey, I'm good. I'm DiMaggio. Look at me." He was very quiet. Was he a mentor to Mantle? I don't think so. That was the only year they had together.

In the years I roomed with Mantle—'54 and '55—they put me in because I was older and more mature. I had no trouble at all with Mickey. He was just a courteous, great teammate. He had some problems with drinking, but not a lot—spotty here and there—as many guys did once in a while. His real problems with drinking, from what I could gather, came after he finished playing and the adulation eroded. He could no longer be what he wanted to be. There was no more of that "Nice going, Mick." And he ended up getting involved with a couple of hustlers and went bankrupt, but he finally came out of it, and nicely.

One of the last times I saw Mickey, I was doing Padres games in Denver. I knew he was coming to the convention center, and I thought I'd go down and say hello. I hadn't seen him in a couple of years. I was trotting down there, and all I could see was fathers with their kids from all directions in Denver heading toward the convention hall.

I got there and told them who I was, that I was a friend, and said, "I'd like to see Mickey." I was told, "Five dollars." I said, "No, I just want to say hello." The guard said, "Five dollars." So I put $5 down. I went into this huge arena with tables just full of baseball cards. In those days the autograph sessions were a big deal. There was a platform down at the end of the hall, and as I was looking around, I heard the crowd let out an "ooh."

Here came the god, walking in. I started to go up the steps, but someone grabbed me by the neck to stop me. Luckily, someone else recognized me and let me in.

When I approached him, I said, "You know, Mick, it cost me $5 just to say hello to you."

He said, "Yeah, it'll cost you $50 if you want a picture." He had 700 pictures and he sold them all at 50 bucks a pop. We did some chatting, but there wasn't much time. I just wanted to say hello.

Mickey was a guy from Commerce, Oklahoma, and New York was his piece of cake—he could do what he wanted to do. He was everything—he was the guy everyone wanted to talk to, the replacement for DiMaggio. Willie Mays had just arrived, but he didn't create the fuss that Mantle did. Willie was probably the better player overall from the standpoint of fielding, but never got the attention that Mickey got. Was it a racial thing? I don't know. It could have been with the public. But athletes don't pay any attention to that. Winning is the bottom line except for an occasional jerk or a real malcontent when it comes to race.

I would guess that the attention Mickey got was overwhelming for him. There is no way it could be otherwise. This is a guy from a town of 2,500 who all of a sudden was thrust into a 10-million population area where he was *the* guy.

Billy Martin and Whitey Ford would become Mickey's best friends on the Yankees. They hung together. I think at the end, they used to get a suite together with two bedrooms. At one time no one but DiMaggio had a solo room. Billy, Whitey, and Mickey had a favorite stunt when they were kids just coming up. They'd get a spray bottle with ice water and spray you while you were in the shower. Nobody was really offended, but they didn't want to get caught in the trap either.

Billy had come up in 1950, and he was a backup infielder that season and in '51. He would take over for me when I went to Korea for most of the following two seasons. When I came back for the full

1954 season, he went into the army. I told him, "I got even with you. I got you drafted."

Billy was a very intense and abrasive ballplayer, but we got along. There was competition between us but not to the point where it affected anything on the field. Billy wanted to out-homer Mantle, which, of course, he couldn't come close to doing. He did hit 15 home runs in 1953, which wasn't bad.

Billy could make the great play at the right time more often than anybody I knew. In the '52 World Series, he made that great catch off a pop-up by Jackie Robinson with the bases loaded, grabbing the ball off his shoe tops. In '53 he singled in the Series-winning run in the ninth inning of Game 6 against the Dodgers and had 12 hits, a record for a six-game Series.

Billy was angry a lot of the time because he wanted to play every day and Stengel didn't always agree. I can't blame Billy since everybody wanted to be in the lineup all the time. That's how it was with the Yankees.

Stengel loved Billy. I think there were only three guys Stengel loved—Berra, Mantle, and Martin. He brought Billy in from Oakland in the Pacific Coast League. I think he felt like his father. And Mantle was the guy I think he wished he was when he was a player. Berra? How could you not like Yogi? Stengel used to tease him a lot.

Martin was a pretty good player and eventually an outstanding manager. I think he patterned himself greatly after Stengel. He had some great years as a manager wherever he went, but he never lasted long. Maybe he was tough to play for, maybe management didn't like him. As a manager, he had a great understanding of the game, but the criticism of him was that he dragged his pitchers way past what they could endure.

Back in the '51 season the New York Giants had stunned the baseball world with their comeback from 13½ games behind the Dodgers in mid-August, winning the pennant on Bobby Thomson's "shot heard 'round the world" playoff home run off Ralph Branca at the Polo Grounds. Mantle, who had been sent down to Kansas City for part of the season, was in right field in the World Series. In Game 2 he was going for a drive in right-center that DiMaggio caught. Mick stepped on a drainpipe and wrenched his knee. He was down, and it seemed as if he were dead. Not even a muscle twitched. Joe said something like, "How are you doing, kid?" By the end of his career, Mickey had sponge wrap on both legs, from his ankle to his groin. I don't know how he could walk.

We beat the Giants in a six-game World Series. By now, I had played three seasons for the Yankees and we had won three World Series.

The next stop for me was Europe. The baseball commissioner's office had asked me to take part in a tour of military bases and talk baseball. Stan Musial went along, as did Frankie Frisch, Dizzy Trout, Jim Konstanty, Elmer Valo, Steve O'Neill, Charlie Grimm, and two umpires. We went to West Germany, England, and Holland.

On our visit to Germany, we went to Garmisch-Partenkirchen, which was the site of the 1936 Olympics. It was bitterly cold, but a gorgeous area.

And we visited servicemen in London and Liverpool. My god, there were acres of downtown London that had been leveled by German bombing. They were still all boarded up, but you could see through the glass they had there. Acres of nothing. The devastation in London was unbelievable. It was as though someone had taken one of these big machines and piled everything out. They still hadn't done much since the war.

I was gone for two months, and when I got back I was exhausted and I never really got into shape. I usually spent all winter conditioning myself for the next year, but I didn't do that this time and I had leg problems when the '52 season began. But there was nothing wrong with my hitting. In a manner of speaking, I was the first .400 hitter since Ted Williams in 1941. I batted .405. But that was for 11 games— my entire 1952 season.

By October 1951 the Korean War had been going on for nearly 16 months. After we'd beaten the Giants in the World Series, I was called over to the Marine detachment at Alameda in northern California. A major in charge there asked me, "What do you think about going back in the service?"

I said, "I hadn't thought much about it."

The major wasn't so much asking a question as making a statement.

"We're going to get you," he said.

"For how long?" I asked.

"A year and a half."

I asked him to do me a favor and take me right away so I would get out in March 1953 and miss only one baseball season. He said, "I'll see what I can do."

My approach was, *Okay, I'll do this and get it over with and I'll come back and start over.* I thought, *If you need me, I'm here.* I've always been that way. I've always felt that your country is more important than anything you do in your private life.

But nothing happened. My request for an immediate call-up didn't get anywhere. I was later told that I would have to report for active duty in early May 1952. I went back to play for the first month of the season because I needed the money. Ed Sullivan put me on his TV show. The theme was that I was doing the patriotic thing by returning to active duty without a complaint although my baseball career was in full swing and I had a wife and two young children. But that hero stuff that Ed Sullivan paid tribute to, the adulation, never appealed to me much.

The Yankees had a going-away ceremony for me on April 30 between games of a Sunday doubleheader with the St. Louis Browns at Yankee Stadium. They presented me with a plaque and a beautiful tea set. I still have them.

What were my feelings on that day? Any time I have to make a speech I have emotions of fear. I hate it. I think most people do, unless you're an egotist and can't stand not to be in front of people. I never needed that. If you look at the group pictures of all the teams I was on, you'll never find me front and center. I would be in the back. I'm not being shy or overly sensitive. I just don't like that stuff.

But I appreciated the tribute from my teammates. I said thank you and then it was off to war once more.

Skies Over Korea

"My prop caught the dirt,
and I was upside down.
My hands were pinned
to my side and my knees
were around my ears and
I was rolled up into a ball.
Suddenly, I thought, *I can't
get the hell out of here.*"

9

Skies Over Korea

I went from Yankees pinstripes to a Marine Corps uniform within hours. The night of that Sunday farewell ceremony at the Stadium I boarded a plane for California and I was soon regaining my pilot skills at Los Alamitos Naval Air Station.

In late May I received a two-page handwritten note that began: "Regardless of the heading on the stationery, please consider this letter as a purely personal one."

The heading read: "Headquarters U.S. Marine Corps, Commandant's Office, Washington" and the letter was from Gen. Lemuel C. Shepherd Jr., the commandant.

He wrote that while we had never met, he was familiar with my baseball career and that he personally regretted that a shortage of pilots had forced me to interrupt it at great personal sacrifice. He also said, "I greatly admire the true Marine Corps spirit that you have displayed since your orders to active duty were issued.... I know that in similar circumstances a man of less character might have protested his orders, made complaints to the press, solicited outside influence, or taken some other action which might have proven embarrassing to the Marine Corps. However, you recognized the realities of the situation, took your assignment like the man you are, and in so doing have proven yourself once again to be a good Marine."

Dan Daniel wrote a piece in *The Sporting News* lauding me, and also praising Ted Williams, a pilot instructor in World War II who had been recalled as well, for serving our country once more. His column bore the headline "Hats Off."

While I was flying attack-plane missions in Korea, Win Elliott, a well-known sportscaster, devoted a segment to me on his Saturday night *Sanka Salutes* program over CBS Radio. As he put it, with an abundance of hokey baseball analogies:

> Little Jerry Coleman was a fancy dan—a brilliant, whirling, graceful athlete who caught the fancy of the crowds. Well, last year Jerry Coleman said so long to baseball. A needed pilot who was being recalled for action in Korea. So little Jerry went, and faded from the sports pages. But this week Jerry was back in the newspapers—and on the front page this time. Coleman still was batting a thousand. On his first two combat missions in Korea, he'd knocked out two vital enemy bridges. Let's remember a hero from yesterday who's more than ever a hero tonight. Let's send Captain Jerry Coleman this Sanka Salute.

Dan Daniel's column and Win Elliott's "Sanka Salute" hailing me as a hero were reminiscent of the tributes I had heard when I came out of World War II and began making a name for myself in baseball. I've never cared for that. I was doing my duty for my country—that's it.

When I went into action in Korea at the end of January 1953, I became the only major leaguer to have been in combat in both World War II and the Korean War. Ted Williams, who, like me, got his wings through the navy's V-5 program in the Second World War, was a flight instructor in Pensacola, Florida. By the time he was about to be sent into combat, Japan surrendered. So when Ted flew as a Marine pilot in Korea—he had jets, I flew prop planes—it was his first time in combat. Lloyd Merriman, an outfielder for the Cincinnati Reds and a great football player at Stanford before that, also flew jets in the Korean War, having been recalled after service in World War II. Like Ted Williams, he had not been in combat then. Lloyd had flown a trainer plane in the V-5 flight program.

Many baseball players—particularly the major leaguers—called into the military during World War II played ball for army and navy teams.

It was entertainment for the servicemen, but there was also a rivalry between the top generals and admirals, all of them trying to get the best major leaguers for their branch of service. There was an Army–Navy World Series in Hawaii, and they rounded up former big leaguers in military outposts all over the world to play in it. Admiral Nimitz threw out the ceremonial first ball.

So when I had been called back to the Marines, along with Williams and Merriman, the sportswriters were saying in effect, "The Marines are trying to get a great baseball team." Well, that had nothing to do with our being called back whatsoever.

When I was at the El Toro Marine air station in California processing for Korea, somebody called me and said, "Hey, I'll give you a couple hundred dollars for a Saturday game." I think it was in Fresno. I said "I'll take it," considering that I had already lost a few dollars in baseball salary and I had a wife and two kids. I drove up there, and somebody took a picture of me. The Marine commandant got a hold of it and he said, "That's the end of this." The Marines were determined to end that talk about recalling ballplayers just so they could play baseball for the Corps. So I only had a couple of games. But it was on my own time. It wasn't Marine stuff, just semipro.

I recall vividly standing in line at El Toro with other fliers who had been recalled after World War II service. Everyone wanted to be an instructor pilot. But they needed us to go into combat.

When I arrived in Korea, I was assigned to fly Corsair attack planes in VMA-323—a Marine Attack Squadron. We were known as the Death Rattlers. The name went back to World War II, when the unit was formed. The story goes that they were in training camp in North Carolina in the summer of 1943 when one of the squadron members killed an Eastern Diamond rattlesnake. Our insignia was a coiled snake perched above the silhouette of a flying Corsair, its propeller spinning.

Corsairs, introduced during World War II and known to the Japanese as "Whistling Death," would carry a maximum load of three 1,000-pound bombs and two 250-pounders, which was incredible for a single-engine attack plane. And they also carried rockets and napalm.

The Corsair was a magnificent plane except on the ground, since you couldn't see in front of you. The nose was really far from the cockpit.

Every military airport in Korea had a number. K-3 meant that the airport was for jets, K-6 was for Corsairs, and K-8 was for night-fighters. I flew off a short runway. If you made a mistake, you had nothing but the end of the runway.

We did a lot of interdiction-type strikes that were not close to the front, attacking a concentration of this, a concentration of that, and all these targets were marked and, I guess, approved by somebody. I remember the toughest anti-aircraft guns in Korea, the .37s. They went *bump, bump, bump*. They probably ran out of gas at about 13,000 feet. But anything between 7,000 feet and 10,000 feet, it was the perfect altitude for .37s. If you had a barrage of .37s, you'd better get the hell out of there.

The worst part of Korea was the jock trip. A jock mission is four pilots waiting to be called. There were times when you would go into the ready room at 6:00 in the morning or earlier and you'd hear a buzzer—"aahrr"—and you'd pick it up: "You're third on the list." That meant that two other groups of planes, other jock troops, had gone out to help someplace, somewhere in the front lines. Sometimes you'd be there all day long until they closed it down; you never knew when you were going to be called. Sometimes it would be quick, sometimes not quick. I can still hear that buzzer—"aahrr"—and you'd drop everything and faint in the process. That was worse than the mission.

What I hated most was to be called on at 5:00 or 6:00 at night, because when you got back it was dark. They didn't have lights on the runways. You had to pick them up and hope for the best.

I flew from a runway about 5,500 feet long, and you were at 20 degree flaps. When you got within about 100 yards of the runway's end, you'd better be in the air or you're done. You'd wobble off and you'd get to about 10,000 feet, and the missions might last for four hours or so.

At night you'd write letters home. A lot of guys hit the club and would end up in the tank if they didn't have a flight the next day. But everybody handled things differently. I used to write a letter home every day. If I had nothing to say, I'd make something up. You never talked about your job, what you were doing.

Marine fliers dropped thousands of tons of bombs in Korea—the authorities would announce the totals—but what the hell good does that do if you can't destroy the target for good?

Korea was kind of tricky. If you were called up to the front and they marked the target with "willie peter"—white phosphorus—you'd knock out this and that and they'd say, "Well, you got about 400 yards of trench." And that night, or the next day, the North Koreans would start work all over again. It was all back to where you left it. Korea was a frustrating war.

They always had four planes circling on the east and west coasts of Korea in case a plane went down on the Korean mainland, and they would try to come in and spot you for a chopper that might get you out.

I had two close calls in Korea—narrowly escaping death each time—and then an emotionally scarring mission when my roommate went down.

On one mission, my radio went out on the way to the target. I was briefed about something like that, so I knew what I had to do. I was to follow the plane in front of me and do my job. I got rid of my bombs. Unfortunately, there were about four layers of clouds, almost like pancakes, maybe 500 feet apart. I was looking for the guys who were bombing so I could join up and come back. I couldn't find anybody. Each layer was empty. I put on my direction finder and honed in to our airfield and managed to get back.

As I was coming in, I looked around and didn't see any other planes, so I made my normal landing. I did not see a Very signal. Usually the tower, if there's a problem, would shoot a Very pistol—it was named for its inventor, a naval officer named Edward Very. It shoots off a flare that's supposed to be visible for a long time. If you saw one, meaning there was another plane in difficulty coming in or taking off, you'd say to yourself, *Hey, get the hell out of there.*

So I was landing—no Very signal in sight—when an F-86 Sabrejet that had an emergency above our airfield came in. Well, I was on the ground and all of a sudden I saw this F-86 hop over the top of me and go down the runway. He was at much faster speed than I was. I was at landing speed. He looked like he could be at takeoff speed. At the end of the runway he crashed into a hill and was killed. I explained to the field that I did not have a working radio. I did not hear anything, I did not see anything. And this guy, of course, was looking for a runway, and we were both there at the same time. Fortunately, he missed me and I'll give him credit for that.

The other near disaster for me came on a takeoff. In the middle of our 5,500-foot runway, you'd hit a little bump. You'd go up and then you'd come down and you'd take off. Well, I hit the bump and the engine stopped—cold. I said, "Oh, god." So I'm braking and squeaking, and now I realize at the end of the runway that I still had momentum. *I'm not going to make it, I'm not going to stop this plane*, I thought. I had three bombs aboard, each of them 1,000-pounders. I let them go. The bombs had wires on them and a propeller, and the propeller had to turn so many revolutions before the bombs were armed—otherwise they wouldn't go off. So the bombs weren't going to explode once they were free of my Corsair. I figured in those split seconds that if I crashed and burned up on the runway with the bombs aboard, I'd blow up the base and myself.

Apparently, one of my bombs hit my tail wheel and flipped me up. My prop caught the dirt, and I was upside down. My hands were pinned to my side and my knees were around my ears and I was rolled up into a ball. Suddenly I thought, *I can't get the hell out of here.*

They always had emergency crews at the side of the runway, and the minute my engine stopped, boy, they pulled out right after me and chased me down the runway. They got to me about as quick as they could before I suffocated, and pulled me out as quickly as they could. But I had passed out by time they got there. The strap of the helmet, under my chin at my throat, was supposed to give ground, but it didn't. I would have died had I been someplace with no help from the ground.

I didn't know what happened until I woke up. I opened my eyes and said, "I think I got a migraine headache." They gave me a shot of something and put me out again. But I was up, ready to fly, at 4:00 the next morning. They didn't give me a week off, I'll tell you that. But I never trusted the Corsair after that in terms of coming down the runway. That's the thing that bothered me most of all about that runway crash. And eventually, things got to the point where they probably worked on me emotionally, because right after that my roommate, Max Harper, got nailed.

We had a tent together, and Max was right across the aisle from me. Max and a fellow named Curley Graves were my closest associates. We were there together for months. Max was a major, a nice guy. Quiet. Had five kids. Wrote to his wife all the time.

One day, we were flying on a mission to hit a target deep in North Korea, and Max hit it nicely. So I dropped my bombs, following him, and we pulled out. All of a sudden I saw smoke coming up from Max's Corsair. His plane did two quick snap rolls. I did a quick 360 to see what happened. By the time I got back, Max had done a lazy eight and was going down.

I sent Mayday calls to those rescue planes off the coastline. They heard me and radioed back, asking if there was any way to help. I said, "There's nothing you can do. There was no parachute. He went straight in."

All I could do was tell the rescue planes the coordinates of where the crash was. I'm sure Max was hit by .37s—anti-aircraft fire.

Seeing Max Harper crash, and my earlier runway crash, affected me more than I realized at the time. I started to hyperventilate and I was missing on my midair join-ups. Not badly, but it wasn't the way I wanted it to be. And I realized there was something going on inside. So they grounded me.

Ted Williams, speaking from the perspective of flying jets in the Korean War, once reflected on my having seen my best friend blow up in front of me. "If it had happened to me," he said, writing in *Officer* magazine, "I would have been useless out there. That was enough to take the starch out of anyone."

On February 16, 1953, Williams had a close call in his own right. He was on a mission near Pyongyang, the North Korean capital, when his jet was hit by enemy fire. His plane was on fire and its handling capacity was in bad shape as he flew back toward a base at Suwon. A fellow pilot named Lawren Hawkins guided him in.

I heard him radioing when he was trouble. I was in the air. You're always on open air on the emergency frequency. So all the pilots aloft at that moment heard, "I've got a Mayday, I've got a Mayday." But we didn't know who it was—we had no clue. When something like that happens, that guy becomes your brother, believe me. It's you that's there and your brother—you're with him all the way. We kept listening. And then we heard, "I got ya, I got ya." Then the conversation stopped. He made it back, but he barely escaped a crash landing.

The next day I found out it was Ted on those Mayday calls. It spread around quickly. I never discussed it with him. You don't talk about those things with another pilot unless he's in your squadron.

Williams was in a squadron together with John Glenn, who went up eventually in Air Force F86s, one of those exchange pilot things. The first time I met John Glenn was when we faced each other on the CBS-TV game show *Name That Tune* in 1957. I didn't know who he was at the time, except that he was a Marine major and he had set a coast-to-coast speed record. The idea on the show was to figure out the tune they were playing and then run over and press a buzzer. I guess they picked me to be with him on the show since I was also a former Marine flier. (That wasn't my only TV game show. I posed as the singer Don Rondo on CBS's *To Tell the Truth* in 1957 and fooled three of the four panelists.)

The next time I saw Glenn was at an affair honoring Ted Williams at Fenway Park shortly after his death. By then everyone knew John Glenn as the first astronaut to fly in orbit, and he had just retired from the United States Senate.

World War II and the Korean War were different animals. Everybody was patriotic in the Second World War. In Korea that was true, too, but we all knew that nothing was happening or going to happen to end the war unless they resolved it at the negotiating table.

My last mission came in May '53. Then they grounded me, with all that tension mounting—particularly the hyperventilation—and I was put in a forward air control unit, living in tents at the front in the DMZ.

"It was my decision," General Vern Megee, the commander of the First Marine Air Wing, told Jim Lucas, a war correspondent, who wrote about my experiences in Korea for the *New York World Telegram and Sun*. "Jerry's got the heart of a lion," Megee said, "and he's done a bang-up job for us. But he's flown his share. And he's had three shattering experiences since he came to us. I decided I owed it to him to keep him on the ground for a while. He'd never have asked it. He's not that kind."

But the fact that I wasn't able to continue flying until my time in Korea had ended has bothered me for a long time. It wasn't until later that I realized the toll it had taken—most visibly the hyperventilation but also a flareup of long-standing stomach problems and a stress-induced loss of depth perception.

My job in those last few months in Korea was in intelligence. I put all this stuff together so night fighters knew where to drop their bombs. Then these planes were all vectored in by a guy on the ground, communicating back and forth. They'd say, "Hit a heading of 180. In about one mile you're going to hit your target. Prepare your drop." The guy would drop his bombs and off he'd go.

On the night of July 27, 1953, following lengthy negotiations at Panmunjom, a truce finally went into effect, ending more than three years of hostilities in Korea. More than 4,200 Marines were killed in the war, and Marine casualties—dead, wounded, and missing—totaled some 28,000. Forty-two Marines had received the Medal of Honor, the nation's highest award for valor, 27 of them posthumously.

I was still in Korea, sitting on a mountaintop, in August when I got a call from Bobby Brown. He had completed his medical studies, had served as an army doctor with an artillery unit in Korea, and was stationed at a military hospital in Tokyo. Bobby told me, "George Weiss wants to know if you can get back." I said, "I don't know."

Ed McMahon, Johnny Carson's future sidekick and a fellow Marine pilot, helped me write a letter and forward it to General Megee. I wrote that I had a month to go on my year-and-a-half tour and I'd be happy to help the Marines get recruits while completing my tour if they'd let me get back to the States so I could finish out the '53 baseball season. Megee said, "We'll have you out in two days."

So this thing was processed back to Washington, and Lt. Gen. Franklin Hart, the assistant commandant, rejected it while Lem Shepherd, the commandant, was away. So there I was, stuck for another month and having to listen to the World Series on the radio. But Shepherd approved my request when he returned to Washington.

I was sitting on my hill and then I heard, "Hey captain, they approved your letter." It took about two to three weeks to get out of the service, especially overseas. But General Megee's sergeant major got me and said, "Give me your piece, you're out of here." I gave him my .38 and he said, "Get going. There's a plane leaving for Japan, a Flying Tiger, in one hour." I jumped on that. I was in Japan for two or three hours, then flew to Hawaii and crossed the Pacific into San Francisco as the only passenger on a mail plane. That kind of thing is impossible unless somebody like the commandant says "get him out of there."

I flew 63 missions in Korea, supporting ground troops and knocking out enemy installations. When you include World War II, that made a total of 120 missions, two Distinguished Flying Crosses, 13 Air Medals, and 3 navy citations. They mention that all the time in accounts of my war service. But I've never counted that up personally. I simply did my duty.

Soon after arriving in San Francisco, I was on a plane to New York, and I rejoined the Yankees in Cleveland at the end of August. But I couldn't play. After my first day working out, I couldn't bend over. Every muscle in my body hurt. I thought, *What am I doing?* I got into eight games—beginning with Jerry Coleman Day on September 13—but I got up only 10 times. It was just a token thing as the Yankees cruised toward their fifth consecutive pennant. The players awarded me one-third of the $8,280 full share for the World Series victory over the Dodgers.

I had left the Yankees at the end of April '52, so I had basically missed two baseball seasons. That's the only thing I wish they'd changed. I had wanted the call-up timed so my 18-month tour would include two off-season periods. Of course, I might be dead, too, you don't know, if the timing were different. But I would have loved to miss just one year instead of the two.

My approach, though, was, *Okay, I'll do this and get it over with and I'll come back and start over.* But I was never really that good again on the ballfield. I left a lot somewhere, somehow, in Korea.

A Yankee Again

"I hadn't realized it, but I was under more pressure than I knew in Korea, and it had lingered, as I was soon to find out."

10

A Yankee Again

Even before the Yankees began spring training for the 1954 season, I worked to get into baseball shape, hoping to regain the form I had before going to Korea. Eddie Lopat had a baseball camp in St. Augustine, Florida, and asked me to be an instructor. They had several hundred young players there, and I tutored the infielders, conditioning myself at the same time. But I made one critical mistake—I put on weight thinking it would make me stronger. It took me six or seven weeks to get into shape as a result, and it slowed my reflexes. I felt heavy. I was up to 175 pounds. I usually played at 165. In my era, we didn't have these special trainers to tell us what to do.

Eddie Lopat had started out as a first baseman. He was a guy who couldn't hit, so he became a pitcher, and he learned the screwball. He was like a Greg Maddux of today, a Preacher Roe of yesterday. They didn't have great stuff, but they knew how to fool you. They'd use their brains as much as their arms. Ed was a marvelous pitcher from the standpoint of getting through a game quickly. If he didn't have the stuff, he was gone in the second inning. But if he got by the second or third inning, he was on his way. Along with Whitey Ford, he was the best pitcher the Yankees had in my era.

Vic Raschi and Allie Reynolds were power pitchers but neither were what I'd call a "pitcher," a guy who sets things up and moves the ball around and uses his brain. By no means were they dumb, but they had that great stuff to overcome inconsistent control.

Raschi was one of the toughest competitors around. In a single year, 1946, he went from Binghamton to Newark to the Yankees. When he made it to Yankee Stadium, he was 27 years old. Almost all the top Yankees pitchers of the late 1940s and early '50s were old, in baseball years, when they started to excel. Ford was the only one who was young and good.

Jim Turner, the Yankees' pitching coach, was brilliant at controlling the pitchers. Casey Stengel made the final calls on personnel, but he relied on Turner a tremendous amount. The people I was closest to on the Yankees were Lopat, Raschi, Reynolds, and Bobby Brown. Raschi and I grew up together with the Yankees; we were teammates at Binghamton.

Most of the young pitchers today are throwers. Greg Maddux is a classic pitcher, and his Braves teammate Tommy Glavine is another. They're what I'd call "professional pitchers"—they don't rely on fastballs to blow the ball past batters. There are a lot of guys just throwing bullets because they have great stuff. Sometimes they last, sometimes they don't.

On the Cleveland Indians of the 1950s, Bob Lemon knew how to pitch, Early Wynn knew. Mike Garcia was a thrower. Bob Feller was a thrower who later learned how to pitch. On the Detroit Tigers, Hal Newhouser was a pitcher; Freddie Hutchinson was a great pitcher. Virgil Trucks and Dizzy Trout were throwers.

In terms of relief pitchers, moving ahead by a few decades, Goose Gossage was a thrower—but a great one. Nobody is a better pitcher among today's relievers than the Padres' Trevor Hoffman. He throws the ball 88 mph at best. Most guys throw it at 90-plus when they're relieving. He knows how to set you up. He's got four great pitches.

Billy Pierce, the Chicago White Sox left-hander, used to drive me nuts with a hard slider that broke in on your fists. Although I had two 4-for-4 days against Alex Kellner, the Philadelphia Athletics' lefty, I never looked at a guy and said "That's my cousin." It was always a battle. The idea was, don't strike out. Today I see guys strike out once every three or four times. As I've mentioned, I struck out once every 10 at-bats, and I wasn't a great hitter.

As for the '54 season, when I returned from Korea, I couldn't hit anything. I had a terrible time. I hadn't realized it, but I was under more pressure than I knew in Korea, and it had lingered, as I was soon to find out.

In July, with my batting average in the doldrums, the Yankees sent me to an eye specialist, and he said, "Are you under pressure lately?" I said, "I don't know." He told me I had lost my depth perception. That was something I wasn't aware of.

My eye problems came from frowning a lot—you basically turn your eyes inward and the muscles don't work properly. That's the way the doctor explained it to me. There's a machine where you take two objects and make them into one, a fusion-type thing. It's a device to help depth perception.

After about three weeks working with it, I was fine so far as my eyesight went. But I didn't get my batting eye back. I played in 107 games in 1954—my first real season since missing most of two summers during the Korean War—but I batted only .217.

The Yankees won 103 games in 1954, but this time we finished second after capturing five straight pennants. The Indians won a league-record 111 games, and they were favored to beat the Giants in the World Series. Then came that great catch and throw by Willie Mays off a drive by Vic Wertz to deepest center field in the Polo Grounds and the home-run hitting of that obscure pinch-hitter Dusty Rhodes. The Giants swept the Indians.

The 1955 season was almost a total loss for me, beginning with a Red Sox game the first week of the season. I was churning around toward home plate in a rundown, and Owen Friend, the Boston shortstop, was about six feet in front of the plate and right in front of me. I tried to crash into him, but he stepped aside like an adagio dancer and I landed on the point of my shoulder. I shattered it in about five pieces. If I had undergone surgery, I would have missed the rest of the year. So the Yankees' orthopedist, Dr. Sidney Gaynor at Lenox Hill Hospital, didn't operate. He massaged it and put the bones in place. He used X-rays to get a guide on how to do it. I've still got a big bump there. It took a long time to heal.

My first game back, the night of July 19 in Chicago's Comiskey Park, I was beaned by a White Sox reliever named Harry Byrd. Harry was just an average pitcher, slugging away. He wasn't throwing at me. Why would he bean me? I wasn't the biggest threat in the lineup. And we didn't even know each other. He threw a fastball that simply got away, and it hit my helmet flush. It knocked me out with a bad concussion. The helmet probably saved me from an even worse concussion, but the beaning put me in the hospital for two days and sidelined me for about a week.

I happened to be wearing a helmet because, coming back after three and a half months sidelined with that shoulder injury, I felt uncomfortable without one. Helmets weren't required, and I hadn't worn one much earlier in my Yankees career even though I had been beaned once before. I was hit behind the ear when I was playing for the Kansas City Blues, and I wasn't wearing a helmet. It affected my equilibrium for weeks. It made me dizzy and upset my stomach. I'd roll over in bed and almost fall out. It did something to those little hairs in the back of your ear. I was out maybe two weeks or so.

Branch Rickey started this helmet thing when he was running the Pirates in the early 1950s. He had a company that manufactured them, and all the Pittsburgh players had to wear them. With other teams, it was a macho thing not to wear a helmet. If you wore one, you were cowardly. Guys called you a chicken if you wore a helmet unless there was some reason. Don Zimmer wore one, but he had been beaned badly. Plus, helmets were uncomfortable.

The guy who changed that concept was Mickey Mantle. When he first started wearing a helmet, everybody picked it up. But Williams never wore one. DiMaggio never wore one. I don't think Musial ever did. Instead of helmets, they used to have pads—little pieces of plastic you'd put in the side of your cap if you wanted to—but they were useless.

I don't think any pitcher I knew would throw at somebody to hit them in the head, but a lot of pitchers would throw up-and-in to get you off the plate, and sometimes the ball would get away. Raschi was an exception. He wouldn't throw at a hitter. His brother was blinded in a baseball incident. He was always afraid of hitting somebody in the head. Reynolds, on the other hand, would brush a guy off the plate.

Today, a pitcher starts fights if he goes inside on a hitter. Years ago, pitching that way was automatically accepted. They'd push you off the plate and then go outside, get you on the corner. A batter who had been brushed back or hit wouldn't charge a pitcher very often. If he did, there might have been a buildup to it. Teams played each other 22 times. Now the Padres play these interleague series where we'll see a team three times and that's it. We play the National League East teams only six times, and the Central teams the same. We play 19 games against teams in our own division. In my era, there might be more animosity between two players because teams met each other so many times. If you didn't like somebody, it could build up. But I never got into a fight with another player.

When you get beaned, generally it leaves a mental scar and you get shy at the plate. Teams look for that. But I was lucky; fortunately I got over it, though I didn't do much at the plate late in the '55 season.

I'm told that I tied a major league record for a shortstop that year by being part of five double plays in a single game. But I don't remember individual feats; there are a few hazy things. What I remember most is winning and losing. That's all that really mattered. The difference today is if you have a good year and you hit 20 home runs and hit .300 you get big money even if you're with a last-place club. That's what the players look for—many of them do, anyway. I can understand it. But we looked for winning. You loved to hit .300 or 40 home runs or whatever, but the key was winning the pennant and the World Series—that's where the money came in, and the glory as well.

The most notable aspect of the '55 season for the Yankees may have been the debut of our first black player, Elston Howard, one of the finest people you ever met. He was a great teammate and a quality person. He'd do anything to help the ballclub.

By 1955, the Yankees were one of the few teams in baseball that had not integrated. The Red Sox were the last team to have a black player, and it took them until '59, when Pumpsie Green, a second baseman, joined them. But the pressure had been building on the Yankees. It was eight years since Jackie Robinson's debut with Brooklyn.

You looked at the Dodgers—Robinson, Roy Campanella, Don Newcombe were the best players they had aside from Pee Wee Reese, Duke Snider, and Gil Hodges. The Giants had Willie Mays, Monte Irvin, and Hank Thompson.

The Yankees had a prime African American prospect in the minors—Vic Power, a first baseman from Puerto Rico who led the American Association in batting in 1953 when he hit .353 for the Kansas City Blues. Power was also gaining a reputation as a stylish fielder, but our co-owner Dan Topping didn't agree. "I am told that Power is a good hitter but a poor fielder," Topping told the United Press in August 1953, while maintaining that "a player's race will never have anything to do with whether he plays for the Yankees."

The Yankees traded Power to the Philadelphia Athletics in December '53, and he went on to win seven consecutive Gold Glove Awards, became a .300 hitter, and made four All-Star teams in 12 major league seasons. He would contend that the Yankees hadn't promoted him because he dated white women and had a reputation as a brawler.

Whatever the merits of that argument, I can say that color in baseball doesn't exist now. It really doesn't. Of course, it did when Robinson broke the color barrier. You had the screwball outfielder in Brooklyn, Dixie Walker, who was going to quit, and the St. Louis Cardinals were supposedly going to strike. The only racial situation I ever came across personally was at Binghamton—the redneck pitcher boasting how he had tried to bean Robinson when he was pitching in the International League. That's the only time I ever heard a racial epithet.

Thank god that stuff's behind us. I don't hear a racial problem now, whether it's Latino, black, Japanese, whatever. I never hear even a thought of a problem with a guy because he's from Venezuela, Cuba, Panama, Puerto Rico, the Dominican. I don't think it exists.

The first year Elston Howard joined us, I was the player representative, and they asked me to take him on *The Ed Sullivan Show*. He didn't want to; they wanted him to go on. The Yankees' addition of a black player was something that attracted quite a bit of attention.

But the Yankees really made a mistake. In 1955, when we had Elston in spring training in St. Petersburg, he had to stay with a private family.

He couldn't stay in the team hotel. I believe that when we played in Baltimore, it was the same thing—he wasn't allowed to stay in the hotel. We shouldn't have allowed that. We just accepted it. We said, "That's the way it is." We should have said, "You won't allow him in our hotel, we'll go someplace else." Those hotels made money on the players, on the teams coming through. That's the one thing I regret as the player rep. We should have stood up and said, "No, he's with us or we're all out of here."

Elston Howard became a key figure for us. He was the American League's Most Valuable Player in 1963, a perennial All-Star, and he hit 167 career home runs. He remained with the Yankees into the 1967 season, catching and playing some outfield. Then, with the Yankees in the doldrums in the CBS era, and Elston being 38 years old, he was traded to the Red Sox. He made it to the World Series that October, catching for Boston's "impossible dream" team. Sadly, he died at age 51 of a heart ailment.

We had won the pennant in Elston's rookie season of 1955 after we were beaten out by the Indians the year before, but this time the Dodgers finally beat us in the World Series for their only championship in Brooklyn. Johnny Podres shut us out at the Stadium in Game 7 after Sandy Amoros made that great catch in left field on what should have been a big double by Berra. We weren't consistent because our pitching wasn't consistent. But the Dodgers had a good ballclub.

I always tease people about the ball that Amoros caught. I say that he never saw the ball, just stuck out his glove and there the ball was. But that wasn't true. He made a wonderful play at a critical time. That was the Dodgers' moment of glory. But we didn't congratulate them after Game 7. We never talked to the opposing players—before the game, during the game, or after the game. Ever.

When the season ended, the Yankees went on a six-week tour of Asia, visiting Hawaii, Japan, and the Philippines. We were formally welcomed by the Japanese prime minister, and we played in Tokyo, Osaka, and Hiroshima.

The night before we opened our exhibition series, 2,000 fans crowded into a theater in Tokyo to welcome us with confetti and fire-crackers. A flower girl gave a bouquet and a dozen soft rubber balls to all the players, and we threw them to the crowd. I introduced my team-mates to the audience.

It was only 10 years since the war had ended. I didn't think about that much in terms of visiting Japan until we got to Hiroshima, where we played an All-Star team from the Japanese Central League and I saw the damage there.

A crowd of 30,000 turned out on a chilly day—we used charcoal heaters in the dugout—and I played a few innings at shortstop, alternating with Gil McDougald. Rizzuto hadn't made the trip.

A precaution had been put in place since, as I recall, we might have been the first Americans to visit Hiroshima as a group. Our team buses had their engines going throughout the game so that we could board them quickly if there had been trouble. Of course, there was no trouble—quite the opposite. Baseball was the national sport in Japan and still is. You can see pictures of us in our caravan. Tens of thousands of people all over the place. It was just like World War II had ended in New York. It was unbelievable. They gave us everything we needed. It was baseball that bridged the gap. They loved baseball and they were so thrilled to see the Yankees, the team of the world, the only sports team with prominence anywhere they went.

I didn't have any bitterness in my heart toward the Japanese, although in Hiroshima I started thinking about a lot of people who weren't here anymore and could have been otherwise. And I'm not talking about Japanese either. I mean the guys we lost in the war.

I was on a popular TV program once—*Tex and Jinx*—and they said, "We'll ask you a question and we'll give you 30 seconds. Would you have dropped the atomic bomb?" And I said, "In 1945, yes; in 1955, no." That was the best way I could answer it. I felt a little more compassion at that time than I had in August 1945. I had returned to the States back then to pick up an aircraft carrier that I would be flying off. I had more than a year overseas; they brought senior pilots back. We were going to hit Japan in November. My feelings in 1945 were *end this thing, right now.* And when we did, who knows how many tens of thousands of lives we might have saved. I was home on leave for a week, and then the war ended.

People forget. The incendiary bombing of Tokyo overseen by General LeMay killed more people than the atomic bombs did. People don't even talk about that. Sure, the atomic bomb was a terrible weapon. It killed a lot of people. But what killed most of the Japanese civilians were the firestorms in Tokyo.

The most important part of my life—and I've said this again and again—has been the time I spent in military service. I reflect on that often. But when the Yankees returned home from Japan in that late autumn of 1955, the images of wartime notwithstanding, more baseball lay ahead for me. I was hoping I could come back from an injury-plagued summer.

Finale for a Golden Age

"I was one of the ultimate team men, as were so many of my Yankees teammates. Having a good year was great, but far and away winning was more important. Winning was everything."

11

Finale for a Golden Age

I started to pick up a little steam and get better after all the problems with coming back from Korea, along with those injuries.

I alternated in 1956 between second base, shortstop, and third. Phil Rizzuto had been released—on Old-Timers' Day, of all things. Billy Martin was starting at second base and Gil McDougald at shortstop, both, like me, from the Bay Area. McDougald had been signed by the scout who signed me, Joe Devine. Andy Carey was the starting third baseman.

We won the pennant again—the seventh time I had played all or part of a season on a pennant-winner—and we got back at the Dodgers, beating them in the World Series, which everyone remembers for Don Larsen's perfect game. Mantle hit a home run to make it 1-0. We got another run, but I always wished that home run had held up to make it a perfect, perfect situation.

One of the sequences that no ever talks about had everything to do with luck. Jackie Robinson hit a one-hop shot to Carey at third in the second inning. It hit his knee and caromed to McDougald at shortstop, and Gil threw Jackie out. Think of the odds of that. With a ball caroming any place except to McDougald, it's not a perfect game. To me that was the greatest part of the perfect game, the fact that Larsen was lucky as well as brilliant.

I didn't get into the game, but I remember the scene vividly. By around the eighth and ninth innings, the players were trying to help Stengel with defensive strategy. Everybody on the bench was saying, "Hey, Casey, how about this guy, should he move over toward right field?" On and on. And Casey finally said, "Goddamn it, I'm the manager. I'll tell 'em where to play."

In those days you weren't supposed to talk about the guy having a no-hitter, let alone a perfect game. Nobody mentioned it to Larsen. He sat by himself, as they usually do in a case like that, but with all the buzz going on around him, he was hardly oblivious. By contrast, Allie Reynolds pitched two no-hitters in 1952 and as he was closing in one of them, he said, "Okay, I got a no-hitter, you can talk about it."

That World Series perfect game produced one of the great images in baseball history—Yogi jumping into Larsen's arms after he threw his final pitch, a called strike three to Dale Mitchell, a pinch-hitter.

In broadcasting, I hear guys say, "The only two hits in the game belong to so-and-so." Well, you know it's a no-hitter, and for the other club. So I tell my listeners that a no-hitter—or even a perfect game—is in sight. Last May, when Greg Maddux was pitching a perfect game in San Diego against Cincinnati, I said just that. It lasted for $5\frac{1}{3}$ innings.

A caller to the Padres' postgame show complained because Matt Vasgersian, who does the San Diego games on TV, had also spoken about the perfect game in progress. Matt certainly had my support. "I think if you're on the bench, you might not want to do it," I told *The San Diego Union-Tribune* the next day when it surveyed our broadcasters about their ways of calling a no-hitter. "But here, the fans want to know."

The 1956 World Series proved the finale for a slice of baseball history. It was the last Subway Series in what has been called the Golden Age of New York City baseball. Every year from 1949, my rookie season, to 1957, my last summer with the Yankees, at least one New York team made it to the Series: the Yankees eight times, the Dodgers five times, and the Giants twice. And only three times in that span was there a team from outside the city in the World Series—Yankees–Phillies in 1950, Giants–Indians in 1954, and Yankees–Braves in 1957.

It was a frustrating time for fans elsewhere on the baseball map. If you rooted for, say, the Athletics, the Senators, the Browns, or the Pirates, the season was over almost before it started. But for New York,

With my Corsair at a base in South Korea.

My Corsair on a Korean runway.

My teammates say good-bye at that Yankee Stadium ceremony. PHOTO COURTESY OF AP/WIDE WORLD PHOTOS.

Casey Stengel ponders my sling after I shattered my shoulder in a play at the plate against the Boston Red Sox in April 1955.

With Phil Rizzuto, my partner on the field and later in the broadcast booth.

Broadcasting for the Yankees at the Stadium in the 1960s.

I've left the San Diego broadcast booth to manage the 1980 Padres. PHOTO COURTESY OF THE SAN DIEGO PADRES.

Maggie and I were married on October 5, 1981, at the Mary Star of the Sea Church in La Jolla, California.

Throwing out the first ball at my 80th birthday celebration in the Padres' Petco Park, September 2004. PHOTO COURTESY OF THE SAN DIEGO PADRES.

With my daughters, Diane and Chelsea, and my son, Jerry Jr.

At my induction into the broadcasters' wing of the Baseball Hall of Fame, July 2005.
PHOTO COURTESY OF THE SAN DIEGO PADRES.

this was the age of "Willie, Mickey, and the Duke," to borrow the title from the Terry Cashman song. It was a time for the arguments over who was the best shortstop, Phil Rizzuto or Pee Wee Reese (though Giants fans might put Alvin Dark in the mix) and who was the best catcher, Yogi Berra or Roy Campanella.

The Yankees would keep winning pennants after that '56 World Series, but by the summer of '58, the Dodgers and Giants were in California, Ebbets Field and the Polo Grounds empty.

In the mid-1950s I took on a job beyond the pinstripes. Allie Reynolds had retired after the 1954 season, and I succeeded him as the Yankees' player representative in meetings with the owners. I didn't run for the job. My teammates voted me in, possibly because I was one of the older players. This was before there was a formal players' union, way before Marvin Miller came along. Back in the 1950s none of the player reps envisioned or fought for an end to the reserve clause, tying players to their teams until they were no longer wanted and giving them little bargaining power.

When I became the Yankees player rep, and later the American League representative for the players, the pensions were meager. We were fighting for better pensions and improved medical and widows' benefits. Bob Feller, Robin Roberts, and Stan Musial were particularly active in that drive. Basically, the money was to come from TV rights. It was a long, tough fight, but we finally pushed it through.

During the wintertime, people like myself who were active in the players' movement never had any time off. We would meet with each other at the winter meetings and we would meet with the owners, the Tom Yawkeys and Phil Wrigleys of the world. Today's players don't really understand how difficult it was. At one time, somebody in management said, "We'll cancel the pension plan." That was the only time up to that point that a strike might have been in the offing. Of course, the plan wasn't canceled—we improved it.

Our leader, so to speak, was a lawyer named J. Norman Lewis. But we fired him because he wasn't helping us. The players had to do just about all the work themselves. Our cause really took off, of course, when Marvin Miller came in, since he was a union man, a negotiator for the steelworkers' union before the players hired him.

The Major League Baseball Players Association was founded in October 1956. Feller was elected president, Musial was the vice president, and I was the secretary while remaining the Yankees' player rep.

In the summer of 1957 I testified before the House of Representatives Judiciary Committee, known as the Celler committee, for its chairman, Congressman Emanuel Celler of Brooklyn. It was looking into the reserve clause and baseball's exemption from antitrust laws.

Like most ballplayers, I accepted the owners' position that ending the reserve clause—creating free agency, as it came to be called—would mean that only the rich teams would win, and it would kill the game. I felt that the reserve clause stabilized the teams and that it was good for baseball that fans knew what was going to happen to their team year after year. The fans knew Joe DiMaggio was going to remain a Yankee, Ted Williams was going to be with the Red Sox, barring an unlikely trade.

Near the end of my testimony, I said that when I was 17 years old, I signed for $2,800 to join the Yankees organization. The war was on and I wasn't even in military service yet.

Celler seemed to think that the Yankees were taking advantage of me, but I said no, the club took the risk because they didn't know whether I could cross the street, whether I could be a big-league ballplayer. And I meant that. And of course they loved me in the Yankees' front office for saying that, I guess, but it was true.

Look at it today. They sign these people for $50 million contracts. The club is always the one taking the risk in a situation like this. Not the player. The player has nothing to offer but his body. Period. The club has to do a lot of financing to figure out how to pay these guys. There are endless amounts of guys—you look them up—who got huge bonuses and never delivered on anything.

I've always felt that when someone gives you something when you're an unproven product, they're taking the risk. That's how I finished my testimony before the Celler committee.

I don't like some of the things I see today. Yes, there were major problems with the reserve clause because you were stuck for life with one team unless your team decided to trade you. Outside of being traded, the only way you could get away from your team is if you dropped dead. But at the same time, it keeps things stable. Let's take Roger Clemens for example. You're a kid growing up in Boston. Roger leaves to go to the Toronto Blue Jays, it's crushing to these fans. They have no idea who's going to be on the team from year to year. I think there should be a balance, but I don't know what that should be.

Over the last 25 years, who's winning all the games? The money teams are winning all the games. I'll bet 90 percent of the winners are the money teams. But one man doesn't do it as it does in basketball. One guy can't change a baseball team. He might make it better but he's not going to win it for you overall. Tom Hicks down in Texas, the owner of the Rangers, he got Alex Rodriguez for $252 million. But where'd they come in when they had him? Last in the American League West, three years in a row.

I think the gains we made in the pension plan during the 1950s were a big plus. The pensions meant financial protection for the players, whether they felt they needed it or not. When you're 25 years old, it seems as if age 65 is the next millennium. For a lot of guys, when they're young they don't really think about needing anything later in life.

I roomed with Mantle for two years so I knew him pretty well. His father died young, two uncles the same. He'd had osteomyelitis, a bone infection. Every time I'd come back from these player meetings, I'd brief Mickey on our hopes for the pension plan. I said, "Mickey, now this was what we got." And he would say, "I'm never going to live long enough to see a pension." He meant it. When he made that statement, "If I'd known how long I was going to live, I'd have taken better care of myself," he meant that, too. I think he believed he had to live as fast as he could.

Now the pensions are huge. And there's also a group called BAT (Baseball Assistance Team) that helps baseball people at any level who can't pay their mortgages. I go to their dinners every year and support them. They help baseball people who are really suffering and struggling, many of them old-timers who have small pensions or no pension at all.

As for salaries, rarely did we know what our teammates made on the Yankees of the 1950s. We had no clue. We knew DiMaggio's salary was $100,000. To this day I don't know what Yogi made or Mickey made. Never asked. Didn't make any difference, frankly. Whatever they got, more power to them. That's the way we approached it. I don't think there's anybody I know who sat in the railroad car on road trips and said, "Hey, that guy's making $35,000, and I'm only getting $30,000."

Mickey was one of the nicest people I've met in my life. Just a beautiful person. But he lost it when he got drunk, although, as I've said, most of his problems came after he retired. They had me room with Mickey in the mid-'50s to slow him down, and there were only a few incidents then. One night before a doubleheader in Baltimore I woke up and Mickey had his head in the toilet. But the next day he went 6-for-8 and I went 0-for-8. I looked at the heavens—it wasn't fair.

Mickey hung around with Billy Martin. "Hey, Mick, let's have a drink," and he'd go along. The Yankees were always concerned that Martin was a bad influence on Mantle. Billy was a tough player in the clutch, but they were afraid he was going to drag Mantle down into the pits unless they got rid of him. Mickey was a guy easily led. They eventually traded Billy because of it. In those days, before no-trade contracts, you could do that.

In '54 and '55, when I roomed with him, Mickey had pretty good years. But he was the MVP when Martin came back full time from the army in 1956. I don't know if my rooming with Mickey helped him much from the standpoint of playing, but we got along great. Of course, he was more comfortable with Billy than he was with me. I was older, a different type.

Mickey weighed 178 pounds when he came to the Yankees and he was 5'10", yet he had humongous power and hit a ball farther than anybody. Nobody ever got down the first-base line faster. He could outrun the damn ball. Because of his skills, futility could make him cry easily. One day he came in and punched a cement wall. He would get so frustrated. I think a lot of people don't know what it's like when you're the guy and don't perform. It tears you apart. It did with DiMaggio, too, only quietly.

Two fixtures with the Yankees during their post-war dominance were the co-owners, Dan Topping and Del Webb.

Topping was a social figure and he had six wives, including Sonja Henie, the great skater. He had a twin-engine seaplane, and Stengel made me fly in it as a copilot. We flew from one end of Florida to the other in spring training. Stengel figured if the pilot had a problem, I'd be there to help him out since I managed to fly in two wars and survive. I spent a little time figuring out which dials did what. I loved it. It was really great. I'd miss all those four-hour bus rides to spring training games, though. I'd get in that plane and hop across Florida in 40 minutes. I do think Casey was uneasy being in that plane. I'd say, "When are we leaving, Casey?" and he'd give me a dirty look. I was the only player aboard.

Del Webb was totally different from Topping. Webb did not have an outgoing personality. He lived on the West Coast, where his other business interests were centered. But I think that when it came down to money, Topping and Webb sat down and discussed it. I don't think that one had more authority than the other. If Topping was going to give DiMaggio $100,000, I'm sure Webb knew it. They'd discuss it on the phone if nothing else.

Del Webb had an office at 745 Fifth Avenue. He was there about half a dozen times a year or so. When I was the Yankees' personnel director in the late 1950s, I worked there, and I never saw anyone go into that office.

Webb hated smoking. If you smoked in that office complex, you'd probably get your head blown off. In those days, remember, if you saw a "No Smoking" sign up, you'd say, "What's this?" As I mentioned, I had stopped smoking in the minor leagues—Bill Skiff, my Newark manager, had saved my neck by telling me how cigarettes sap your strength—but I did do cigarette and pipe advertisements. They paid you.

The Saturday Evening Post ran an advertisement showing me puffing on a pipe. It read: "Jerry Coleman, star second baseman of the New York Yankees, says: 'Nicotine will never get two strikes on me. I've switched to Medico Filtered Pipes. Now I throw away all the nicotine that's trapped in the throwaway filter and I enjoy pipe smoking more than ever.'"

I was at a banquet once with Bill Skowron, our first baseman, and someone asked him about smoking. He said, "I'd eat 'em if they paid me."

In the summer of 1957 I was alternating again between second base, shortstop, and third base in what would be my last season as a Yankee. That spring I witnessed one of the most horrific scenes on a baseball field—the Herb Score injury.

Herb was a great left-hander with the Indians. He had led the league in strikeouts in his first two seasons and he was only 23 years old. Then, on a May night in Cleveland, Gil McDougald hit that line drive that struck him right in the face.

I was on the bench, and we all went out. I took one look and said, "Oh my god," and walked away. There was blood coming from his mouth. It was such an incredible set of circumstances. I don't think I've ever seen anybody get hit like that. It was unbelievable.

Gil was crushed and he started to cry. It stayed with him emotionally. He never got over it. It wasn't one of those "breaks of the game" things. And the injury destroyed Herb Score's career. He was never that good again. Eventually, he became a broadcaster.

That's the worst baseball injury I ever saw, except for one in New York where a shortstop from Cleveland and an outfielder collided and the shortstop suffered serious head injuries. The other one I saw in San Diego a couple of years ago when Mike Cameron and Carlos Beltran of the Mets collided in the outfield.

Those were three baseball injuries that shook me.

May 1957 proved to be an eventful month. A week after the Herb Score incident, the Yankees were making headlines off the field—not exactly the kind that the club wanted. The action was at the Copacabana nightclub. Billy, Mickey, Yogi, Hank Bauer, and a couple of other guys were celebrating Billy's 29th birthday when a customer got into a fight with Bauer. It made all the papers, and soon after that Billy was traded to the Kansas City Athletics, putting him about as far away from Mickey as you can get and still be in the major leagues.

I was invited to that party, but I didn't go. I don't recall why. The sad part about the Copa thing was not the scramble with whomever they were fighting but the fact that they signed Dan Topping's name to the check. The Yankees fined the guys for that.

I played with Hank Bauer on the Kansas City Blues and with the Yankees for years. He wasn't the kind of guy you'd want to pick a fight with. He had been a gunny sergeant in the Marines. I know he was wounded at Okinawa. As a fellow Marine, I used to kid him: "It was pretty stupid to be on the ground, where they're shooting at you."

Hank was a great, great competitor. He never walked anyplace. Always ran. He had trouble with the curveball, and certain right-handed pitchers ate him alive, but overall he was a fine hitter and he had one of the greatest arms in baseball out in right field, although he didn't glide around the way DiMaggio did. But then, who could?

Hank was a good professional player and a tough and fast base runner. If Hank was on first and the ball was hit to the shortstop and he threw to second base, Hank would get to second and break up the double play. And he had power. I think he hit more than 20 home runs as a leadoff man one year. He was a good manager, as well. You know who was the first Baltimore Orioles manager to win a World Series? It wasn't Earl Weaver. It was Hank in 1966.

As for the Copa fracas making headlines, you had sportswriters everywhere. There were 10 newspapers in New York when I got there, and each one had a writer that followed the club, and then you had the Associated Press, United Press, and International News Service. And you had two newspapers in New Jersey, two on Long Island. When you took batting practice, there must have been 20 writers around the cage.

Some of the sportswriters stayed with a club 15, 20 years. They knew the players, you knew them. You knew whom to be comfortable with and whom not to be. Dick Young of the *Daily News* was a marvelous writer, but you also knew that he was dangerous at times. He was a very aggressive writer, going for the throat in that sense. John Drebinger of the *Times* was a pretty nice guy. Some other names were Will Wedge, Dan Daniel, Dan Parker, Arthur Daley, Red Smith, Ben Epstein, and Til Ferdenzi. Ferdenzi was very loyal and easy to work with. He knew what to do and what not to do. Some guys could be trouble. You didn't know them the first week. It took a while.

When you talked to a writer off the record, you had to know who you were dealing with. One of the disappointing moments of my life in terms of dealing with writers involved Dan Daniel, who worked for the *New York World-Telegram* and covered baseball for many years. He asked me, "Who do you think the commissioner's for, the players or the owners?" And I said, "Well, the owners pay him. I guess he's got an allegiance to them to a degree, I guess he's their guy. I don't even know." It was off the record.

The story was sort of tilted toward "the owners control the commissioner, and the commissioner controls baseball." Dan Daniel gave the story to Dan Parker, the sports editor of the *New York Mirror* for many years, who printed my remark. Dan Parker wrote it as if he had talked to me. And I didn't want it written. I never forgot that, and I never forgave Dan Daniel. That, to me, is unconscionable, to give an off-the-record comment to another writer. So I've had trouble, so to speak, totally trusting some writers.

That being said, dealing with the media is more difficult for today's players. You blink and some kid just out of college says, "Well, what'd you do today?" Crazy things. Some of the questions are unbelievable.

Some guy stuffs a microphone in your face, you don't know who he is. Or you get a phone call, "Hey this is Joe Blow, from a sports show in Toledo." They come at you from all directions.

I got to know Howard Cosell well. My family and his—he and his wife, Emmy, had two girls—socialized at each other's homes and we spent nights in Howard's house. Of course, he was a broadcaster, but very much like the writers in New York. They were very, very plugged in to what was happening. In fact, Howard changed broadcasting by going to the heart of the story and not wishy-washing around it. He was a very bright guy, a brilliant man.

He was also a lawyer. I remember he said, "Can you get me Mickey Mantle's account?" This was before he became a big star in broadcasting. I said, "Well, I'll talk to him." He wanted Mantle's financial dealings, as an accountant, to do whatever you do with those things. He later said, "Don't ever get me Mantle again." Mickey wasn't financially bright, I guess, or didn't pay a lot of attention—let's put it that way. And he drove Howard nuts—Howard was trying to figure out his income tax.

Howard was a very honest man, but was also totally insecure. Tragically, his Jewish background hurt him a lot because he used to get frequent hate mail. He carried a newspaper article that said "damn the Jewish people."

Emmy and his daughters were his life. When she died, he went with her.

My playing days were nearing an end in the summer of 1957. I played in about half the games that year, mostly at second and third base. I had never tried to hit one over the Green Monster at Fenway Park, but in my final regular-season game I drove a home run over it, off Frank Baumann, a left-hander.

We won yet another pennant, and the Milwaukee Braves came in first in the National League after all those years of Dodgers and Giants domination. We lost to them in a seven-game World Series, but I played second base in all seven games and hit .364, the leading batter in the Series except for Hank Aaron. I singled off Lew Burdette in the ninth inning of Game 7 with the Braves up by 5-0. That's the way it ended. Burdette won his third game of the Series, and it was the final base hit of my career.

Although I had played well, we lost, so it was a bad Series as far as I was concerned. You look back and you try to remember, *What did I do, did I hurt the team?* I never found things I did well. I always found things I did wrong. Could I have done it differently? I always examined my approach to the game and what I did during the game.

Was I too hard on myself? Probably. But I think you have to be if you're going to get good. You always look to make yourself better. I was one of the ultimate team men, as were so many of my Yankees teammates. Having a good year was great, but far and away winning was more important. Winning was everything.

Beyond the Diamond

"People look at ballplayers and the others in the game—managers, coaches, executives, broadcasters— and it seems like a charmed life. You're getting paid handsomely to fulfill every boy's fantasy. But what the public doesn't see is the life beyond the ballpark, the toll that baseball can take on families."

12

Beyond the Diamond

Although I had a fine World Series in 1957, the Yankees envisioned Bobby Richardson as their new second baseman when the following spring arrived, and I was headed for a backup role at best. George Weiss offered me a job in the front office.

I had nine years with the Yankees. If I didn't take the job, there was a risk I'd be traded. I had a home and a family in New Jersey and I didn't want to move. I thought, *What the hell, I'm not going to get any better, and I'm 33 years old.* I was among only three Yankees on all of Casey Stengel's eight pennant-winning teams, six of them World Series champions. But it was time for another kind of life in baseball, and I took the job. But as it turned out, the demands of my executive job would keep me away from that home in New Jersey.

I became the personnel director for the Yankees. We had maybe 10 farm teams, and my job was to staff all of them except for Richmond of the International League, whose players were chosen directly by the Yankees' front office. I provided the players for teams in Class A, B, C, D, and Double A, and I had four scouts under me. I wanted to be a major league general manager eventually.

But a problem developed—George Weiss wouldn't spend the money. Weiss was what I'd call a money man—he liked baseball, but he liked money better. I always felt—although this was just a rumor—that if he beat the budget he was given by the Yankees owners, he received a commission. He could never survive in today's market without changing his mind-set. But in those days teams had control over players. Players had no options.

So the Yankees missed the Frank Howards, the Ron Fairlys, the Tony Cloningers, the really top-flight prospects because they were getting $50,000 and we were offering $5,000, $10,000, something like that. We wouldn't compete at that level. That's where the Yankees started going downhill. The press and public have given Steinbrenner the what-for all the time—"the Boss," that sort of thing. But this guy has kept the Yankees name up front. I know he spends a lot of money, but he created a winning situation.

We competed for prospects with our name in the 1950s. I did sign Jim Bouton, and I was there when Joe Pepitone was signed. But generally speaking, when other teams came in with big bucks, the Yankees name didn't mean anything to kids.

To get a promising prospect, in addition to offering the money, you had to do some stroking. Ron Fairly owes me $300 in lunches. I scouted the University of Southern California team he played on, and he was a good hitter. I took him for lunch and dinner often, but he had already been signed by the Dodgers. We didn't even know it. He went on to play in the major leagues for 21 seasons, but none of them with the Yankees.

At first I worked for Lee MacPhail, and then he went to the Baltimore Orioles. Then Roy Hamey came in, and that's when I knew I was in the wrong job. Hamey asked me to go out and follow our minor league teams in Portland and Modesto. Portland was getting into the playoffs in the Pacific Coast League. I watched them play the Spokane Dodgers, who had Frank Howard, Tommy Davis, and Ron Fairly—a big ballclub with lots of potential stars. From there I went to Modesto, our Class C team in the California League. I watched them and compiled five pages detailing all of the talent. But when I got back to New York, Hamey never called me and asked me about it, never checked my write-up. I think he just wanted to get me out of New York. He didn't want me in the way. I think I may have posed a threat to him.

And the job was very difficult for my wife, Louise, and our two children. About January 1, I headed out to the West Coast, where they played baseball all winter long, and I worked with the scouts. And from there I went to spring training in mid-February, and then I went back to Florida in late April for extended periods with players in the farm system. At times I'd bring my family down there and put the kids in special schools, which was difficult.

Once the season got under way, you'd visit every farm club, just bouncing around. They'd open up at different times and they'd never stop. And, finally, the killer was that they had the rookie league starting just after the major league season ended. That would take you to about November 1. I loved the work, but it was devastating for my family. We were living in Ridgewood, New Jersey. My daughter, Diane, was nine years old at the time, and my son, Jerry Jr., was seven. Louise had to cope with raising the children while I was on the road. In 1959 I was gone 223 days up to October 24 or 25. It was a desperate situation. I realized that I couldn't continue this way.

People look at ballplayers and the others in the game—managers, coaches, executives, broadcasters—and it seems like a charmed life. You're getting paid handsomely to fulfill every boy's fantasy. But what the public doesn't see is the life beyond the ballpark, the toll that baseball can take on families.

When I was going to Lowell High School, I met Louise Leighton. She went around with one of my friends, and I went around with one of her girlfriends. I was home on leave in 1945, I'd just returned from the Pacific, and I went to Seals Stadium to watch a game. Lo and behold, here comes Louise walking by with a boyfriend. I said, "Hey, Louise, how're you doing? Let's have lunch." She was just a friend then. I never thought about the romance part of it. But we started dating and we eloped in February 1946. Then we had a big wedding that fall.

She had long dark hair, beautiful eyes. She had everything. But she should have married a guy who went to work at 9:00 in the morning, got home at 5:00 PM, had a month's vacation, that sort of stuff. Our life was always fractured. There was never any stability or continuity to it. I had a flaw—I was climbing mountains. And unfortunately, when that happens, you're busy doing things—gotta be there, do this, that, and so forth, and always out there running around like a lunatic. She needed a more stable life.

You take a young girl and put her into the baseball atmosphere, into New York and into Yankee Stadium, there are a few moments of delight, but mostly she's alone while I'm running around the country playing baseball and attending dinners all over the place.

We had a wonderful home, a son and a daughter, and everything going for us, but you have to be a certain kind of person to tolerate that sort of personality in your partner who's always out there struggling and fighting and running around in circles.

Louise's father owned a chain of cafeterias—Leighton's—all up and down the West Coast. He was a very wealthy man and a very prominent businessman, the first guy who developed cafeterias out there. And then the crash came in '29. He went back to six or seven restaurants in the San Francisco area. The family lived in St. Francis Woods—*the* place to live.

But Louise's mother had a drinking problem. Louise started to drink, too. I was an enabler. I didn't even know what I was doing. I said, "I'll get you a bottle of vodka." But she was getting a lot of bottles of vodka.

Moving ahead some years, long after we had moved back to California, her problems became so serious that I had her set to go to the Betty Ford Clinic in Rancho Mirage for whatever it took to get her straightened out. I don't think we'd gone out of the house together in five years. She was pretty much in the house by herself. I said, "Look, Louise, you've got to get this done."

She had been fading, but I didn't sufficiently understand this then. I should have recognized that she needed somebody to take care of her. And I finally thought I was going to get it for her, going to Betty Ford. But the night before she was supposed to leave, she wouldn't go. And so I said, "Well, that's it," and I left. We both moved out of our house. I bought a condominium for her near Diane, elsewhere in San Diego, and we divorced not too long after my time managing the 1980 Padres.

Louise couldn't surmount her problem. Early in 1982, she took her life. She overdosed, over-drugged, took too many pills. She was in her fifties, but at the end she looked way beyond her years.

My daughter Diane is still living in the San Diego area. I admire her greatly. She's a marvelous teacher and she made a grandfather of me.

In the fall of 1968, when I was still broadcasting for the Yankees, Diane went west, enrolling at California Western University in San Diego to pursue her goal of teaching. She later received a master's degree in counselor education from the University of San Diego.

She has been teaching in the San Diego area for more than three decades, most recently on the fifth-grade level, and has counseled high school students. Her daughter, Courtney, formerly worked for the Pittsburgh Pirates, helping arrange promotional events like fantasy camps, and is now working at Point Loma Nazarene University in San Diego. Diane's son, Christopher, is in the insurance business. Diane has given the ring that I gave to Louise, a beautiful square-cut diamond I bought in 1945, to Courtney, for the day she gets married.

Jerry Jr. has worked in the hotel business. People might ask if I had hoped my son would become a baseball player or encourage him to pursue that. The answer is no. I've felt that whatever my kids wanted to do was okay with me. I would tell them, "What's your aim? Go for it."

I passed on the motto that was related to me by my mentor Frank Crosetti: "You never give in—you never give up." I would tell them how they're going to be disappointed. Dozens of times, hundreds of times. Who knows? It happens to everyone.

When Jerry Jr. was in Little League, they'd say, "Would you go out and play second base like your dad?" I thought, *Oh, god. He wasn't a good baseball player. They should never have done that to him. Put him in right field or anyplace but there.* People don't understand that.

The only two players I know who have succeeded past the expectations of their fathers are Ken Griffey Jr. and Barry Bonds. All the rest of them, no. It certainly wasn't that way for Mickey Mantle's kids. When I was the Yankees' personnel director, we signed Charlie Keller's two sons, mostly because of his name. But they didn't make it in baseball. Pete Rose's kid has played in the low minors past the age of 30. It's too bad. The kids can't necessarily be what their fathers were.

And I wasn't Jack Armstrong, the all-American boy. All my buddies used to call me that because I didn't drink, didn't smoke, but I look at old pictures of me and I think, *How the hell did I ever get to the big leagues?*

I was skinny, scrawny, weighed 160 pounds, and I had no power at the plate. I was a gifted fielder—that's what kept me with the Yankees.

As for being the child of a well-known father, Diane says that she has adored me from day one and considers me her best friend. But as she puts it, "I don't like to talk about my father in terms of who he is. I don't go around thinking that my father is this and that. He's simply my dad."

Back in 1960, with the toll on my family from all that traveling and all the pressure, as a ballplayer and then the Yankees personnel director, finally catching up with us, I was hoping for a more settled life. Then Howard Cosell, my good friend, came in one day and said, "If you weren't going to be the next Yankees general manager, have I got a job for you."

"I beg your pardon?" I said. "Let's talk."

Van Heusen, which was a white-shirt company at the time, was going into sportswear. They had hired ex-athletes like Rocky Marciano, the Dodgers' Carl Erskine, the baseball Giants' Jim Hearn, and the football Giants' Sam Huff and Andy Robustelli to promote their clothing line. Howard Cosell brought Van Heusen to my attention and I came aboard. I took the job because I wanted to go back to the West Coast, where Louise and I had our roots. The idea was that I would be Van Heusen's representative there. Unfortunately, Carl Erskine had a child with Down syndrome. Carl was going to work for Van Heusen in New York, but he decided that his hometown of Anderson, Indiana, would be a better environment for his family. So Van Heusen asked me to stay on in New York, which I did.

I started learning the shirt business. I had meetings, for example, with the guys out in Wilkes-Barre, Pennsylvania, selling the Van Heusen line to various store owners. I really worked at it hard.

I also did a few things for Van Heusen on the West Coast. Lefty O'Doul was a big favorite out in San Francisco, and he and Joe DiMaggio were bosom buddies. I set up promotional displays with them at Golden Gate Park and elsewhere. They loved it and made a lot of money from that. Lefty, of course, was a San Francisco native and had managed the Seals for many years, and, I believe, once had a chance to go to the big leagues as a manager. But he was doing so well with the Seals and making probably as much as he would in the big leagues, so he stayed there. Back in the 1920s and early '30s, he was one of the best hitters in baseball, playing the outfield for the Giants, Phillies, and Dodgers. (I should note that he made his big league debut as a Yankee.) He later opened a restaurant and bar in San Francisco across the street from the St. Francis Hotel, and it became a hugely popular spot.

While working for Van Heusen, I found a totally new career. CBS-TV hired me in 1960 to join Pee Wee Reese and Dizzy Dean for *Game of the Week*. I got the job through Bill MacPhail, who was a member of a leading baseball family—a son of Larry MacPhail, a former part owner of the Yankees, and a brother of Lee MacPhail, my boss in the Yankees' front office for a while. Bill and I became friends while he was the traveling secretary for the Kansas City Blues when I played for them in 1947. Then he went into broadcasting. He had tried to hire me as a broadcaster at CBS right after I had taken the Yankees front office job, but I felt I couldn't leave the Yankees after I had said yes to that. He hired George Kell, the former third baseman, instead.

Two years later I called Bill and asked if he was still willing to hire me for CBS, and he was. So I went to my Van Heusen people and said, "Would you mind if I did weekend games?" They were happy to allow it—it would promote me and promote my association with Van Heusen, too.

When my playing days had ended, the last thing on this earth I had ever thought about was becoming a broadcaster. I'd never been on the air before—no training, no nothing.

My job was to do the pregame interviews for CBS, though eventually I broadcast a few games when Dizzy or Pee Wee took time off.

When I wasn't at the ballpark, I did outside interviews. My tape recorder was the size of a suitcase, not one of these tiny things you stick in your back pocket today. You had to have an engineer go with you to work that thing when you went out on a story. It was reel to reel—those round things. It drove me nuts. You had to carry all this baggage. You couldn't just jump in the car. If so-and-so was at the Waldorf-Astoria in Room 756, you had to go into the studio, get this guy, get the equipment. By that time, you could be in China. If you had that thing in hand, you could go anyplace you wanted very quickly.

When it came to interviewing at the ballpark, before Dizzy and Pee Wee broadcast the games, I didn't know what I was doing.

For my first interview—with 25 to 30 million people watching in living color—I didn't know where the microphone was. The floor manager counted me down—five minutes, four and a half, and so on. Then finally when he pointed to me, my knees turned to mush, and I had Red Schoendienst as my guest. I looked to Red—the longtime St. Louis Cardinals star infielder, later their manager, and eventually a Hall of Famer—and said something very inquisitive like, "How's it going, Red?" He talked for five minutes, and finally the floor manager said, "Wrap it up." I heard the guy in my ear saying, "Throw it back, throw it back." I said, "Now back to Pee Wee and Dizzy."

I came close to hugging Red on the spot for helping me get through that first interview.

One day, I was doing the pregame show with my guest Cookie Lavagetto, the former Brooklyn Dodgers third baseman who was managing the Washington Senators at the time. They played the national anthem just after we began chatting. Well, I didn't know what to do. I wondered if the audience could hear it. Should I keep going, should I stop? I had a dumb director who was dumber than I was and should have cut me and hit the flag. Period. He's the guy who should have taken charge because I didn't know what to do. I talked all through the national anthem, and CBS got a lot of letters. My military background saved me. Today, if I hear the national anthem, I stop mid-stride wherever I am.

In July 1990 there was incident in San Diego involving Roseanne Barr and the national anthem, and it became a national story. She had been invited to sing by Tom Werner, the Padres' chairman, who was also the executive producer of her *Roseanne* show. She hyped her singing it to the point where it was insane. People started to boo, and the more they did, the crazier she got. When she ended, she spit and grabbed her crotch, imitating a ballplayer. That went over even worse with the crowd. Her husband, Tom Arnold, said afterward that she had trouble with an echo from the sound system. But of all places to do that sort of thing, San Diego, being a military town, was the worst choice she could have made.

Getting back to my CBS days, Dizzy Dean was still a very prominent personality in this country at the time I worked with him and he'd been a real character, going back to his days as a great pitcher for the St. Louis Cardinals teams of the 1930s—the Gashouse Gang. I used to listen to him in Korea when he was doing the Saturday Game of the Week on radio, and he had also broadcast for the Cardinals and the Browns and briefly for the Yankees. He put on a show with his mangled syntax and his barefoot-boy charm. Dizzy's runners didn't slide, they "slud." When Pee Wee was describing the action, Dizzy, having ballooned to nearly 300 pounds, might warble "Wabash Cannonball," an ode to the Norfolk & Western railroad train that rumbled through the border country.

He came out of the Ozarks, the son of a sharecropper, and he had no education to speak of. But he knew exactly what he was doing at all times. He was a very bright person. He wanted the image of being the good ol' boy, sort of stumbling around. But he wasn't. He was a very sharp person. No question about it. And he knew what broadcasting was all about. He knew who he was and how to do it, and he did a great job.

Dizzy hated to fly. We did two games a week, one Saturday and one Sunday. Once in a while we had two games in the same town but very rarely. I think we were leaving St. Louis once to fly to Baltimore on one of those old three-tailed props. We went down the runway, and all of a sudden, *bing, bing,* the lights and signals go on. The pilot was coming to a screeching stop, saying something like, "Ladies and gentlemen, we have to go back. There seems to be some kind of a problem with our outboard engine." So we went back. The pilot said, "We'll have this taken care of in a little while. We'll go into the ready room. We'll call you when we're ready to go again."

The passengers eventually all got back on the plane, except for Dizzy—he disappeared. He went home. His fear of flying took over. Pee Wee and I ended up doing the next game by ourselves.

I recall one of the last times I spoke with Pee Wee. We had a big sports banquet, and I called him and said, "Pee Wee, we'd love to have you come out and be our guest speaker." And he kind of hemmed and hawed. He said, "I don't know if I'm going to be able to make it." He had cancer. He was dying and I didn't even know it.

I also did CBS Radio's *Game of the Week* on Saturdays, beginning in the mid-1970s, while I was broadcasting for the Padres. I stayed with that for 22 years. Every week, virtually every Saturday game I did was on the East Coast. I'd take the 11:05 PM flight out of San Diego on Friday. It always stopped in Chicago, and then I'd go on to Toronto or New York or Baltimore, for example. And then, if I was broadcasting a Saturday afternoon game, I'd come back later in the day. If I had a Saturday night game in New York, I'd get up at 4:00 AM Sunday morning, run to the airport at 5:30 AM, get on a 6:00 AM flight, then go through Chicago and into San Diego, and the only thing that saved me was the three-hour time spread. I'd get off the plane and then do a Padres game Sunday afternoon. I never missed a game in San Diego that I was supposed to do because of a plane problem.

I always thought, *Gee, if I could just do more West Coast games for the CBS Game of the Week, that would be great.* So I'd get a game in San Francisco. You know where the Padres were that weekend? In Pittsburgh or someplace in the east.

I had a dramatic role as a broadcaster, playing myself in Billy Crystal's made-for-TV movie *61**. It recalled Roger Maris's record-breaking season and the controversy, created by Ford Frick, the commissioner at the time, as to whether Roger should truly have been considered the home-run king since he played in a longer season than Babe Ruth had. (In fact, there is no asterisk in the record book.)

I think it was Roger's home run number 50 that I "called" in the movie. It was done in a Los Angeles studio, and Billy was tenacious about getting the scene right. I did that call maybe 25 times before Billy got what he liked. I was beginning to think, *Come on.* But I had a chance to chat with Billy, who is a huge Yankees fan, and he was a nice man. A perfectionist, obviously. I've never seen the movie on television—it appeared in 2001—though I saw some of the early releases of it. A lot of the language was overdone, I think, to make a point more than anything else.

Roger and I were pretty close, and I recall working with him in 1961 when I was still with Van Heusen, putting on promotions all over the country while doing the Game of the Week for television on Saturdays. One of the promos was in the New York area, and it included Roger along with Bill Skowron and Whitey Ford. We were to do it one day in early May when the Yankees were scheduled to be off. But the day before there was a rainout, and that game was put off by 24 hours, to the day scheduled for the promo, so we had to cancel.

We looked through the entire schedule to find a compatible date and settled on September 26—it was somewhere around there. We had to go to Long Island for it. Roger had 59 home runs at the time. You can imagine the chaos that would be surrounding this. He was staying at some place off the green in Central Park. I went down there and said, "Look, Roger, if you don't want to do this, I understand."

His hair was falling out, the pressure was so intense. He was having an awful time. But he said, "Don't worry about it. I'll do it. I'll be there."

We went to the shopping center on Long Island and there must have been 10,000 people there—I'm not kidding. It was so bad they went through the windows, shattered them. We were standing on a four-sided platform, and the microphones went out to only two or two-and-a-half sides, and behind you couldn't hear. Every time Roger stood up, they went crazy, started to roar and scream. You couldn't get anything done. We finally needed the police to get us off the platform.

Roger was a delightful person. Years later, when he moved to the Gainesville, Florida, area, I was going to buy a radio station down there with another fellow. I called Roger. He picked us up in the morning and shepherded us all over town and stayed with us through the whole thing, then put us back on a plane and sent us on our way. He had no financial interest in this—he was just doing us a kindness.

I was at an old-timers' game in 1985. I didn't like playing in those things when physically I couldn't really play anymore. But I went. As I was looking into my clubhouse locker, this arm went around me and grabbed me by the neck and started to choke me. It was Roger. I hated high school hijinks in the clubhouse. I said, "For god's sake, leave me alone, you turkey." I could talk to him that way because he was a friend of mine. Then I said, "How are you doing?" He said, "Well, okay, but I got another lump here."

There had been an article in the newspaper about the cancer he had. That was the last time I saw him. He was dead within six months. I wrote a letter to his wife, Pat, telling of my feelings for Roger. I think he was great, and with all that's gone on with steroids in baseball, in my opinion he still has the single-season home-run record.

After my third year with CBS, Ballantine beer, which sponsored the Yankees games, invited me to broadcast for them. I was happy to say yes. So I quit Van Heusen. I tried to keep my CBS-TV job for Saturday games, but the network wouldn't let me. Now it was back to Yankee Stadium, this time behind the microphone.

With Mel and Red and the Scooter

"For Mel Allen, and I'm
sure with Red Barber,
working with Phil and
me had to be a problem.
They were professional
broadcasters. We were a
couple of ex-jocks."

13

With Mel and Red and the Scooter

When the Yankees began spring training in March 1963, I immersed myself in play-by-play broadcasting for the first time, and I had quite an introduction to that. They had me at the mic for a game at the very beginning. I was going to do one inning. I said to myself, *Oh my god, three ground balls to the shortstop, let's get it over with.* Well, 12 men came to the plate, and everything that ever happened in a baseball game happened in that half inning. I was beside myself because I didn't know how to keep score. I didn't know what I was doing. But I staggered through it. And finally Mel Allen came over and said, "Jerry, I think you've had enough." I said, "You're right."

Except for a couple of play-by-play broadcasts, I'd confined myself to the pregame or postgame programs on *Game of the Week* for CBS-TV. Now viewers and listeners would be comparing me to the most prominent professional broadcasters in the business, Mel Allen and Red Barber. Phil Rizzuto, the Scooter, my double-play partner, was also part of the broadcast team, and Joe Garagiola later replaced Mel and stayed for a while before going to NBC.

Howard Cosell tried to make a broadcaster out of me. He went into the ABC studios and worked with me, and I was lousy. Frankly, no broadcaster should start the way I started. It's absolutely wrong to start a guy at the top and make him do play-by-play when he doesn't know how to speak or keep score. I look back on it now and say that's unfair. You should start people in the minor leagues. Ease them in.

Kids ask me all the time how long it takes to become a big-league broadcaster. I'll tell you what, if you go to bed with a dictionary, if you study every aspect of the ballgames, take the rule book, study that, then maybe in 10 years you might know what you're doing.

Incidentally, I have never patterned myself after another broadcaster. I explained my thinking at a news conference when I was inducted into the broadcasters' wing of the Baseball Hall of Fame in 2005. I put it this way:

> I find it's better in my opinion not to listen to anybody else broadcast, because what you are is what you are. And if that doesn't make it for you, nothing else will. So consequently, I've never even listened to other broadcasters. I've tried to stay completely out of that realm. In fact, the first time I heard myself, I was doing shows for CBS, and this goes back to the early '60s. I was going across the George Washington Bridge—I lived in New Jersey at the time. I heard this program, I almost turned off the bridge and jumped. It's very hard for broadcasters to listen to themselves and be anything but critical.

The worst thing about broadcasting is that you're public fodder. My first year with the Yankees, somebody mailed me a phonograph record called *Jungle Sounds* and wrote "Listen to yourself." Isn't that a great way to make you feel good? Well, nobody's good when starting out. I've been lucky, frankly. And baseball is the only sport I have really liked to do. I've done UCLA basketball, I've done bowling, boxing, golf, many of the other sports. I never liked those things at all.

In my first season broadcasting for the Yankees, I only did road games, filling in for Red, who didn't travel with the team. I got a little bit more proficient, finally, where I knew what I was doing. But it was trial and error.

Looking at it now, the way they set it up was rather insane. There would be a week where Phil and Red worked together, Mel and I worked together. The next week, Phil and Mel would work together and I'd work with Red. We did this all year long. But within each game, we'd do half on radio and half on television. So you had four voices doing radio games, four voices doing TV games. The mishmash was incredible.

Rizzuto and I worked together a lot, and people liked us because we were a couple of characters and we weren't the serious-type broadcasters that Mel or Red were. I still get letters: "I remember when you and Phil...." It kind of surprises me. There's a thing about a baseball fan—and I can say this from being in the game since the early 1940s—once a fan, he remains a fan for life and never forgets. There are good people out there.

I used to get letters saying things like, "Why don't you do this? Why don't you do that?" I haven't had that sort of thing in years. Anyway, if you walk into a room of a hundred people and say, "Hi, my name is so-and-so," before you even open your mouth, many of them will say, "I don't like you." You're on the 50-50 mark to start, and then you've got to work on the others. You're public and you're going to get people who take one look at you, don't like your style, don't like the way you look, don't like anything about you. That's part of the game. But when you're new in it, you don't understand those things. It's painful at times.

After broadcasting for 45 years or so, I don't worry too much about that sort of thing. Basically, you like to appeal to people, you like to make them think that you're doing well. But believe me, you're not going to do it all the time. The only guy you have to worry about is the guy who hires you.

Since I had no instruction, no nothing, it was just what I could feel in my own being that kept me going early on with the Yankees. So something was almost sure to go awry.

I had an experience in Cleveland during a doubleheader. Birdie Tebbetts, the old Red Sox catcher, was managing the Indians, and it was my job as the junior guy with Mel and Phil to go down and get the names of the starting pitchers. I said to Birdie, "Who's pitching?" He said, "McDowell and Kralick"—a pair of left-handers. I thanked him and didn't question him any further.

We were going through this first game and I was saying, "McDowell's got a wild streak, but he's looking good today." Jack Kralick was a spot pitcher with pretty good control. Sam McDowell was erratic and wild but a great strikeout pitcher. Suddenly here's McDowell looking like he's a control freak, spotting the ball here and there.

Finally, in the fourth inning, we get the message from WPIX-TV in New York, which was carrying the game: "We think that's Jack Kralick, not Sam McDowell."

Bob Neal was broadcasting the game for the Indians to my left. I said—off the air, of course—"Bob, who's pitching?"

He said, "Jack Kralick."

So then we had to inform all our viewers that we were announcing the wrong pitcher for four innings. I'm in the baseball record book: "Most innings wrong pitcher, Jerry Coleman."

It was just a crazy set of circumstances. Professionals don't make mistakes like that. But Phil and I—a couple of dumb ex-jocks—thought it was a riot. Well, someone had to tell Mel that we had the wrong pitcher. We had Bill Guilfoile, the guy who kept our stats, do it. I saw him whispering into Mel's ear, and Mel put his head down on the desk—he didn't come up for two minutes. He realized what a disaster it was.

I'll never forget the day Phil and I were doing our all-time Yankees team: in the outfield, Mantle and DiMaggio and Maris. Somebody called in and said, "What happened to Babe Ruth?" You talk about the phones lighting up. I thought, "Oh my god, we forgot Ruth." So we had to apologize.

Phil and I had a very warm relationship playing and broadcasting. He was a delightful guy. And his skills in the field, of course, had been enormous. It seemed as if he never made a bad play. He was one of the best right-handed bunters, along with Dom DiMaggio, I ever saw. He could hit, he could steal bases. He was a great player.

For Mel Allen, and I'm sure with Red Barber, working with Phil and me had to be a problem. They were professional broadcasters. We were a couple of ex-jocks. Red was a great teacher. He didn't take to Phil because Phil was "ww"—wasn't watching—and he'd leave early in a game. Red, who was a very strict person that way, felt that Phil took his broadcast job too casually, that he didn't have the proper discipline in his approach. Phil was what he was—a great personality. I got along great with Red. Mel got along with everybody.

One thing that Red probably didn't tell me was "keep your pants on." I had an exciting moment during a broadcast in Kansas City on a sizzling and humid day. There was a catwalk about 20 feet long between the television and the radio booths. After you finished with TV or radio, you would walk to the other booth to do that segment since we switched around. On a very hot afternoon, we would take our pants off to try to stay somewhat cool, and in Kansas City we would run across the catwalk in our undershorts. When we were on TV, even if the cameras were put on us, you couldn't see our lower halves. So I had done this, and I was sitting down, happily doing a game, when all of a sudden there's a strong hand on my shoulder. It's a cop. He said, "Put your pants on." How could I? They were in the other booth. A woman in the stands had complained. I didn't think my legs were that bad.

Red took me under his wing and he taught me things that I've used to this day. He told me about broadcasting's ground rules, you might say. He told me never to go into the press box unless I was asked to do so. When I started broadcasting at Yankee Stadium, there was a huge expanse of chairs for writers and there was a little step that went down to the press box. The broadcasters were not allowed in the writers' section, even though it was right around the bend from our booth. It was out of bounds. We stayed in our own little bucket. Except for Mel Allen and a few others, broadcasters were just beginning to become prominent people. The press, I think, was jealous of broadcasters because they were making so much more money than the writers were. I think they resented it. Now, half the writers have become broadcasters because it's a much easier way to work and a much better way to make money.

Red told me what to eat, what not to eat: "Don't eat anything mushy or creamy or sugary before a game. It'll make it hard to talk."

And most important: "Make sure, Jayee, that you know something is right when you say it. There's no guessing in this game—you got to be right."

The way he said it was, "Jayee, Jayee." Jerry was Jayee—kind of a southern lilt.

As for our interacting on the air, Red told me, "You can talk when I ask you a question."

My response was, "Okay, Red, whatever you say."

Red was in charge. But he brought me in a lot. "What do you think of this, Jayee?" he'd ask. And I'd tell him what I thought. Over the years, I've worked with a lot of guys who are not even my peers and won't talk to me.

In his memoir, Barber wrote that he had problems with Joe Garagiola interrupting him, stepping on his lines. Joe did talk a lot, there's no question about it. But at the same time, you understand what your partner does and how he does it, and you work around it. Is he a color analyst? Joe did that a lot. Joe was good and he was probably the most underrated broadcaster in the business. He was kind of a folksy guy, but sharp as a tack. You wanna know what goes on in baseball, Joe can tell you. And he always left it with a humorous tone.

The Barber–Garagiola issue aside, a lot of people think that by talking, it makes them better. It doesn't. Sometimes you talk too much and you irritate people. You have to know what the balance is. I'm less of a talker.

Red was fired after the 1966 season. CBS had bought the Yankees from Del Webb and Dan Topping and put Mike Burke, a show-business executive, in charge. Burke, I thought, was pompous. I didn't like him. I think he was more of a flamboyant front guy but didn't know much about baseball. He promoted himself more than anything else.

Red went to breakfast with Mike Burke one day and came out without a job, and he was really crushed by that. We'd won the pennant in '64, and then Yogi was fired as manager after we lost to the Cardinals in the World Series. Then we hired the winning manager, Johnny Keane. Soon after that came the long decline under CBS, and we were 10th in a 10-team league in 1966. Red thought the story of a game late in the '66 season was the lack of attendance at Yankee Stadium. He kept talking about it—Yankee Stadium with 413 people in the stands. And it certainly was a big story. But the Yankees didn't like it, and Red was fired. Red, of course, was hugely popular in Brooklyn before coming to the Yankees, but he left the Dodgers after having his differences with Walter O'Malley. Red was a stubborn guy but a brilliant broadcaster.

The best broadcaster, of course, was Mel Allen. He had the voice and the clarity. I never thought Red had a broadcaster's voice, personally. But he was far superior to any of them intelligence-wise.

Mel was the Ballantine beer man, and I was the Ballantine ale guy in commercials between innings. When we were doing them on TV, they'd turn the cameras on us. While you were doing the commercials, they might change players and you didn't even know who was in the game. Now, of course, the commercials are on tape so you don't have that problem.

When we did them live, Mel Allen would gurgle down Ballantine beer in those small arrow-shaped glasses. At the end of some of the games he wasn't quite solvent. I'd hold beer or ale up to my lips. I couldn't drink. It would make me hiccup.

I had one commercial session in Chicago doing Ballantine ale. I was presenting it, and some guy—I have no idea what his name was—was drinking it. We were there for literally nine hours doing a set of these. About the eighth or ninth hour, this guy got so drunk he fell off his seat and we had to stop.

They had hired me to keep Mel off the air a little bit because they were getting complaints that he talked too much, that he never shut up. I didn't pay much attention to that. I didn't know anything about it. But I recall vividly how they tried to keep Mel out of talking for nine innings, which he used to do all the time. Especially when the team was on the road. There was no Red Barber, and he would just dominate everything.

One day, in Baltimore, there was a rain delay. When that happened, we didn't send it back to the studio. We looked for people to interview. I was on the air when the rain started, and Mel sat down next to me. And he'd wobble back and forth when he wanted to talk, and I said something like, "What do you think, Mel?" And two hours and 20 minutes later he stopped talking. He talked through the entire rain delay, and I think that was the straw that broke the camel's back.

There was a very weird situation involving Mel trying to be of help to Mantle in '61, when Maris set the home-run record and Mickey hit 54 homers. Mickey had a cold or a virus. Mel took him to his own doctor, which is a no-no. You never administer medicine that the club doesn't know anything about. The doctor gave Mickey a shot in his hip, and that got infected and he missed the last week or so. The Yankees later found out about Mel's doctor. "How'd you get this?" they asked Mantle about his infection. And the story came out. Why Mel didn't get fired for that I'll never know.

One time, Mel disappeared from our broadcast team in Detroit. They said that he'd fallen in the bathtub and hit his head, and he was not doing well. It was never clear what that was all about. In 1963, while he was doing the Yankees–Dodgers World Series with Vin Scully, they had to take him off the air because he couldn't talk. It wasn't his voice—it just wouldn't come. That finished him professionally. He was fired after the '64 season, and Garagiola took his place. But Mel was a marvelous broadcaster. He was the dominant sports broadcaster of his time.

Another fixture at Yankee Stadium—and he's still there, with his perfect intonation—was Bob Sheppard, who has been the public address announcer since 1951. I can still hear him: "Playing second base, Jerry Coleman—Coleman at second base." Nowadays most guys on the PA systems are projecting themselves, trying to gain attention, and they give the home team that extra inflection. I find that annoying and I don't pay much attention to it. But if that's what the people like, it's okay by me.

Casey Stengel was certainly a fixture at the Stadium, and then after the Yankees lost to the Pirates in the 1960 World Series on Bill Mazeroski's Game 7 home run, they fired him. This guy won 10 American League pennants and seven world titles in 12 years, and they said, "We need a change." How do you like that? So they brought in Ralph Houk. He turned out to be a fine manager and won three more pennants and two World Series titles, then moved up to general manager and turned the managing over to Berra.

Yogi won another pennant. After the Yankees lost to the Cardinals in a seven-game World Series, I was walking down Fifth Avenue. Yogi had a meeting with the Yankees front office in Midtown, and I almost knocked him down going around the corner.

I figured he was receiving a contract extension, and I asked him, "Hey, how many years did you get?"

"I got fired," he said.

I think that was a major mistake by the Yankees. Players lose a World Series for you. Yogi's great comment was, "What makes a great manager? Good players." And it's true.

Johnny Keane, the Cardinals' manager, replaced Yogi, but he was the wrong man for the job. He was completely miscast. New York is a special place to manage in, a very difficult situation to exist in, and if you can't do that, then you can't manage there. Keane was a wonderful person, but it ate him alive and he died of a heart attack early in '67. But Yogi's managing days weren't over. He went on to manage the Mets for a few seasons—won a pennant with them in 1973—and later managed the Yankees again.

Yogi was very shy. One of the reasons he was not a more successful manager was he couldn't communicate his thoughts to the players. And you've got to work with the newspapers as well in New York. Stengel was a great talker, but Berra was not, and therefore it was more difficult for him. But Yogi was a very bright person. For some people, he had the image of not being bright, but that's not true at all. I consider people smart or dumb depending on how good they are at their profession. He understood baseball, he understood players. He never made a mistake on the ballfield that I ever saw. He knew how to play.

As for the famous Yogi-isms, I can attest to two. When Yogi was honored at a game in St. Louis, his hometown, he told the crowd, "I'd like to thank you for making this night necessary." And when Bobby Brown was reading a medical textbook, Yogi asked him, "How did it come out?"

Mantle, like Berra, wasn't a Phi Beta Kappa, but, like Yogi, he never made a mistake on the baseball field. Joe DiMaggio had a 10th-grade education, but he never made a mistake. Some guys who are college educated don't do well at all. They don't know how to react.

It's a weird business. Being an athlete is sizing up a situation in an instant and reacting. Some guys can and some guys can't. I also think that Yogi took a bad rap because his physical appearance didn't lend itself to being a scholar.

Ralph Houk was very bright and a gung-ho tough guy. He won a Silver Star in the Battle of the Bulge and by the end of World War II he was a major. That became his nickname. And he was a great competitor as a player, though he was the Yankees' third-string catcher. He got into only 91 games in eight seasons with the Yankees.

After all that success as the Yankees manager, he figured he could do the job as general manager.

When you take someone from a managing job and make him a general manager, the public may not realize it, but you have to set up an entire operation that includes hundreds of people. It's very hard to suddenly become a general manager and know all the ins and outs of everybody in baseball. You have to have scouts in the field, minor league managers, coaches. It isn't just, "I'm the general manager, I'm going to make this trade." It's an immense job.

I think for Ralph that might have been tough, as it would be for anybody to have been a manager and then suddenly become a general manager. You've got to have somebody who knows what's going on in every part of the United States. Ralph did okay as a general manager, but basically he was better off as a manager.

Of course, he went back to the dugout for many years, becoming the Yankees' manager again when he fired Keane early in the 1966 season. But he never won another pennant with the Yankees or, after that, while managing the Tigers and the Red Sox.

It wasn't all baseball for me in that turbulent decade. In 1967 I was asked by the baseball commissioner's office if I'd go to Vietnam and entertain the troops. I said, "Sure. Who's coming?" They said, "We've got Pete Rose and Joe DiMaggio." I said, "Well, you don't need me."

But I went, and Tony Conigliaro, the outfielder with the Red Sox who later got beaned badly and ultimately died young, went along, too.

When our baseball troupe got to Vietnam, it was only Joe DiMaggio the troops wanted to see. Nobody cared that the rest of us were there. Joe's magnetism was incredible. Once, in the middle of the night, Martha Raye, the comedian who was really devoted to the troops—they made her an honorary colonel—marched into our sleep-in. "Hey, you goddamn dago, where are you?" she roared. She woke us all up, looking for DiMaggio. Joe was the guy everybody wanted to see whether they were 19 years old or 99.

We got out around Christmas, about a month before the Tet offensive, which changed the entire look of the Vietnam War. People in this country and the military realized we weren't going to win this thing. Here were the people who were supposed to be defeated and weren't. All we heard about were those body counts. Well, we killed 3,000 here and there, but we weren't winning. When I got there, I realized Da Nang was an enclave. We had enclaves all over the place, but we didn't control the countryside. I wasn't used to that kind of war. I was used to front lines.

We went through every hospital in and around Saigon. Guys sitting on beds with blank stares on their faces, with head injuries. When I got back from Vietnam—I was living in Ridgewood, New Jersey—they asked me to come to an auditorium one night to speak about the trip, about the war itself, and there were several hundred people there. Somebody said, "Are we going to win?" I said, "The best you can hope for is a tie."

Even still, I never saw as many awful wounds until I went to Walter Reed Army Hospital and took at look at some of those soldiers from Iraq. A while ago, I visited the hospital with a few Padres players, including Trevor Hoffman, our star relief pitcher. I think that Sandy Alderson, our chief executive officer and a former Marine, set it up.

I was there on the fringe. The players were the ones the soldiers recognized. I was like their grandfather, like Methuselah as far as they were concerned. But the fact that I was there, they appreciated it. Otherwise they sit in a bed all day long.

There were so many horrendous wounds. The whole side of a leg with a big gash down it. No legs at all. The thing that was so beautiful to me, they brought the families in and boarded them while the wounded were being taken care of. We kind of isolate the casualties. We don't think about it.

They talk about the number of deaths in Iraq. There are so many thousands of injured personnel, too. These kids are just incredible. They have a bounce to them and a smile to them. I saw guys with no legs laughing and smiling—can't wait to get out there, get started again. At least up front they sounded okay. I guess they're happy to be alive. But they'll never be whole again. Who knows how good they'll be for the rest of their lives?

"Hang a Star"

"Do you know what
'throwing 'em up in
the bullpen' is? That's
playing catch. You say,
'He's throwing 'em up,
playing catch.' Someone
maintained that I said
that 'so-and-so was
throwing up in the
bullpen.' I responded by
saying, 'Well, if you had his
stuff, you'd throw up, too.'"

14

"Hang a Star"

After seven years as a Yankees broadcaster, I wanted to get back to my West Coast roots. I was interested in broadcasting for the Padres, but they didn't have an opening, so in 1970 I took a sports broadcasting job with KTLA-TV in Los Angeles.

I alternated on the nightly sports news with Tom Harmon, the former Michigan football star and a decorated Army Air Forces pilot in World War II. While I was there, Howard Cosell called and asked me if I'd like to be the sports genius out in California for the ABC radio network. I told him, "Of course I would." So I was working about 10 days a week.

In addition to my KTLA program, I did shows every weekend on ABC. I'd go into the studio and spend all day there. There would be live shows on Saturdays and Sundays and features on Sundays, too. I'd get there at 3:00 or 4:00 in the morning, and I'd update all day long—three-to-five-minute specials every two hours. I used to go out and get interviews, but some were done on the phone. I was calling Notre Dame or Dartmouth or whoever was in the news, getting those quick cuts, and then talking around it. That lasted for three years.

In 1972 I got the job I wanted in the first place—broadcasting for the San Diego Padres, who had been created as an expansion team in '69. Buzzie Bavasi, the Padres' general manager, who had been the Dodgers' general manager in Brooklyn and Los Angeles, gave me the job. I've been there ever since.

☙ • ❧

I have two trademark calls with the Padres.

"Hang a star" is rather personal. I couldn't spell very well as a youngster, and when I was in grammar school, every Friday we had a spelling test of 20 words. If you got them all, you got a gold star. I never got a gold star, and I consider that to be the epitome of excellence. I am the official ordainer of the star. It's for an outstanding defensive play. And, of course, nobody else can use the star because it's mine. Its circumference is around two feet and it's on the end of a broomstick. When it's time for the gold star, I poke my engineer and he sticks it out the broadcast booth. Above the press area, they have my name with a star beside it.

KFMB radio, which used to do the Padres games, once gave out "Hang a Star on That One!" membership cards to fans in the team's colors of the time, yellow and brown. "When you see a great Padres play, help Jerry Coleman 'Hang a Star on That One,'" the cards read. They instructed fans to face the radio broadcast booth with arms raised and to hold it there "for a minimum of five seconds" to signal a great play. The cards could be worth a variety of prizes, and fans were asked to "listen to KFMB Radio for details."

My other call—"Oh, doctor!"—is an exclamation for anything special on the field, and it came from Casey Stengel, who used to say, "Get what I mean, doctor? You got me, doctor?" One day, just out of the blue, I said, "Oh, doctor!" on an extraordinary defensive play. Red Barber had used the expression when the Dodgers' Al Gionfriddo made that great catch to rob DiMaggio at Yankee Stadium in the '47 World Series. But I didn't know about that the first time I exclaimed "Oh, doctor!" I think Red used it only once.

It was in the early 1970s with the Padres that my first "Oh, doctor!" came out. It just erupted, and it's been there ever since. A lot of broadcasters spend time thinking up good catchphrases. I've worked with people who have done that. They practice. I never think that way.

There's another term that's associated with me—"Colemanisms," or what you might call flubs. I talk fast, and maybe I talk too quickly, too soon.

I may have said the one on Winfield: "Winfield goes back. He hit his head against the wall. It's rolling toward the infield." I meant the ball, of course. I just didn't get around to saying "it wasn't his head rolling toward the infield." I skip a word here and there.

Somebody claimed that I said, "He slid into second base with a standup double." What happened is, when you pop up at second base, it becomes a standup double. But I forget to tell them, "Well, he slid, and now he's standing up."

Here's one that may not be on anyone's list, but I'll confess to it. I was broadcasting a Phillies game nationally with Jack Buck. Mike Schmidt was playing third base. As I mentioned, I talk fast. I said, "Ground ball to shit, he's up with it, over to first. He's got it." At the end of the inning, when we were off the air, Buck remarked, "You know you just said 'shit.'" I said, "I know—for the third time."

Here's a so-called Colemanism that really isn't. Do you know what "throwing 'em up in the bullpen" is? That's playing catch. You say, "He's throwing 'em up, playing catch." Someone maintained that I said that "so-and-so was throwing up in the bullpen." I responded by saying, "Well, if you had his stuff, you'd throw up, too."

All this has been well recorded for years. I don't pay any attention to that stuff.

As for how I call the game, I'd point to the citation when I received the Hall of Fame's 2005 Ford C. Frick Award for excellence in baseball broadcasting. It said I had "a very concise style." That's pretty much true. I can say something in one sentence it may take some guy half a paragraph to get through. I don't think you should belabor things. The game is what's important. It's on the field. And for me to sit here and tell you "this is the pitcher's second time out; the first time he went $2\frac{2}{3}$ innings, gave up three hits, a walk, struck out two...." Who cares? I'll say "he's had a couple of bad outings" and I let it go that way. That's just the way I do it, personally. Everybody's different.

In broadcasting for the Padres, I don't dwell on my years with the Yankees. I try to stay away from that "remember when" stuff because it wears people out. I'm a Padres broadcaster. If something hits me, it has to be spur-of-the moment stuff, like, "Yeah, Mantle struck out

1,700 times, for heaven's sake. Reggie Jackson set a world record striking out 2,500 times. That's five years of not hitting the baseball." And then it's over. That's one thing that bothers me about some ex-jocks—they live in the past. They've been successful as athletes and then their lives end. I know there are some of these great ex–Hall of Famers who drift around, taking bows for the rest of their life. How dull can it get?

As for former ballplayers in the broadcasting business, unless they're real jerks, they have trouble criticizing players on the field because they feel self-conscious about it. It's difficult to be critical because they know how hard it is, and they have friends on the field. It's hard to say "he misjudged the ball and blew the game" when you first start to broadcast if you're an ex-player. You have great empathy for what goes on out there.

And there are plenty of reasons that someone doesn't catch the ball: maybe a bad hop, the sun, or the fielder didn't get a quick jump off the bat. Who knows? If there's an error to be made, I made it at one time or another. It's easier now for me to say "he should have caught the ball" than it was 30 years ago.

If a guy boots a ball in the first inning, the only run of the game, and his team loses the game, I don't repeat it and repeat it. If I criticize a player, it's not because he's a bad guy but because he misjudged something and didn't make a play. That's the end of it. I don't go back to it. I might say, "I think he had trouble finding it." I don't say, "That turkey out there, that's the fifth game he's blown for this ballclub. I don't know why he's on the team."

I don't have a problem with pointing out mental errors. There are reasons to be critical, and you can talk about those kinds of things, but to lay on them for nine innings is a waste of time.

Outside of mental errors, one thing really bothers me: when a batter takes a fastball down the middle for strike three with runners on base. Unless he didn't see the pitch, why can't he swing at the darn thing?

I've worked with almost all the broadcasters in the business over the past four and a half decades. Lindsey Nelson was one of the best. I flew to Japan with him, and we did two Japanese league games in 1981, when they had the long players' strike and the split season. We were broad-casted back to the United States. KTLA in Los Angeles handled it.

Before the games, we were waiting for the lineups. Twenty minutes before the games were to start, they brought them—in Japanese. We had to get somebody to decipher the names, and we certainly couldn't pronounce them. Lindsey saved the day. He was a real pro.

My wife, Maggie, who made the trip with me, was there for some amusing moments in Japan. So I'll let her take it from here:

> We were hosted by the Nippon Broadcasting Company, and some parts were hysterical. They took us out to dinner in Tokyo. For starters, I'm 5'10", and at the time I had red hair down to my waist practically, so I got lots of stares. Then it became clear to me they didn't know what to do with a woman in this broad-casting situation with all these executives.
>
> They took us to a place where they grill food right in front of you. The PR guy, who wore golf clothes all the time, stood up at the beginning of dinner and said, "People from California are vegetarians, so we need to know if anybody's a vegetarian." We said we weren't, and he said, "Good, because this place special-izes in Kobe beef."
>
> They seated me in the place of honor next to the president of Nippon Broadcasting, who had spent a little time in the United States. He basically spoke no English and I spoke no Japanese. So we were working really hard to have a conversation, and it was difficult. We were all seated around the grill. And then I felt Jerry poking my other side, and he pointed at the grill and said, "Look at their eyes." I was thinking, "I don't want to look at their eyes, whatever it is." I didn't see it coming, but they had brought out a big oval cop-per platter with giant prawns that were not only raw but alive. Their eyes were going back and forth. They

dumped them on the grill and they started jumping around. The producer from KTLA said, "I hope that's not the way they cook the beef."

The prawns were right in front of me. I was so surprised, I started going, "Oh, oh, oh," and backing away from the table, which gave everybody a good laugh. Then they collected them all under this copper hood, and you could hear them banging around. And then they served them—heads, feet, everything.

What we didn't know was, in order for them to stop giving you food, you have to leave a piece. We were trying to be good Americans in eating everything they gave us, including the head and the feet, and I was thinking, *My god, I'm going to die.* So the prawns finally ran out. Then they brought out giant clams and sea scallops. Everything was raw, alive, and gigantic. And they cut up every little bit of it.

So that's how Maggie and I spent part of our strike-induced vacation.

As for baseball broadcasting over the years, a lot has changed—if not drastically in terms of style, then in the sheer number of voices. When I broke in with CBS-TV in 1960, their Game of the Week was the only one televised nationally. Now there are 50 stations. Everybody is broadcasting games. And they have so many broadcasters, you don't know who half of them are except for the guys who are on locally. You have 30 teams, and some of the teams have six or seven broadcasters. At one time you had two. The Yankees had only three in the early 1960s—Allen, Barber, and Rizzuto—and then I came aboard because Red didn't want to travel.

I watch ESPN, ESPN2, I see different guys every day. I don't know who these guys are. I don't even have a clue. At one time, you knew every broadcaster in the country and who they worked for. Growing up, I listened to Ernie Smith, the voice of the San Francisco Seals. I don't remember any other broadcasters helping him along. Now it's become a golden job for ex-jocks in any sport to be a broadcaster.

I grew up as a broadcaster on TV and I did both television and radio for years until I went solely to the radio side, which I prefer. On television you see something but you've got to get the director to pick it up for you. It's a slow mechanism. You're talking about some bird that's flying across the field, the director has a picture of some woman holding a baby. You're always at the mercy of the director because he's got to get to what you want to talk about. Another thing is, you're listening to the director in your earplug. It can be irritating to have some guy talking to you while you're talking. But usually when you work with a director over a period of time, it gets easier because he's following you and knows what you want. My first director on TV was Jack Murphy with the Yankees. He was great—helped me a lot. "Calm down, calm down," he'd tell me.

Radio is a medium for baseball more than television is because you can create the image, create the situation, create what's going on and stay with it.

The trouble with television is, people see what's going on. You might say, "There's a ground ball to shortstop. He's up with it, over to first, he's got 'em." People can see that.

But on radio, it's, "A ground ball to shortstop, ooh, tough hop, he's got it, over to first, just did get 'em in time." On TV you don't need that because they see it. A fly ball on TV, you may wanna follow it and you're not going to say, "There's a long drive to left field, there goes the outfielder chasing it." Well, people are watching the outfielder chasing it. It's a totally different animal.

My eyes were giving me trouble a couple of years ago, and the worst experience I ever had as a broadcaster was when the ball would disappear from me every now and then. I've had that corrected now, and I've got 20/20 vision. I see better than most broadcasters. At that time, it was fading a little bit. I called strike three and it was a home run. That was embarrassing: "Oops, sorry folks, it was a home run and not a strikeout." What can you do except correct it?

As I mentioned, my mother was nearly blind in her final years after a long battle with glaucoma. I take drops in the morning and the evening, and I have no trouble with my eye pressure, but I still see a specialist twice a year.

I've had two great moments in baseball. One was my first pennant with the Yankees, when Birdie Tebbetts of the Red Sox popped out to Tommy Henrich for the final out on the final day of the '49 season. The other was the Padres' pennant victory in 1984.

When I joined the Padres' broadcasting crew in 1972, the team had been bad since it entered the National League three years earlier. Before free agency, it was hard for a new team to become competitive quickly.

The first year I was in San Diego, the attendance was about 600,000, and the Padres nearly moved to Washington. But then Ray Kroc, who made his fortune creating the McDonald's dynasty, bought the Padres early in 1974. He had grown up in Chicago and tried to buy the Cubs a few years earlier.

Kroc made quite a splash immediately. In the Padres' home opener, we were losing to the Houston Astros 9–2, had made three errors, and committed a base-running blunder that killed a rally. We were about to come up in the eighth inning when Kroc barged into the broadcast booth. He said, "Where's the microphone?" I said, "Down there, Ray." He wanted the public-address mic.

I said to my engineer, "If he starts talking, pick it up, will you?" And he did.

"It's the worst team I ever saw in my life," Kroc told the crowd. "I'm embarrassed. These guys are terrible and awful." He went on for about three minutes on how lousy the Padres were, and in the middle of that, a streaker ran across the field. Well, the people loved him for it. Because here was the owner who was just as mad as they were about what was going on.

After the game, Doug Rader, who was playing third base for the Astros, came to the defense of the Padres, saying that Kroc "must think he's in a sales convention, dealing with a bunch of short-order cooks." The next day, Rader got long-distance phone calls from cooks, complaining they had been demeaned by him, and he made an apology.

We finished last in the National League West in '74, just as we had every season since the team was created, but we drew more than a million fans, almost twice the home attendance of the year before.

Ray Kroc was deaf in one ear. He came to Chicago once and they wanted to put him on the air. I was sitting on the left side and he came in and sat in the right-hand seat. I said, "Ray, this and that and the other." And then I left, and Bob Chandler, my broadcast partner, came in. Bob was in the seat to the right of Ray, who was deaf in his right ear.

Chandler asked some questions, and all Ray could say was "Eh? Eh?" He didn't know what the hell Chandler was talking about.

Ray was a volatile person, a brilliant person in his business, of course. I think he was like a lot of owners, impulsive: "Get rid of that guy."

In 1980, when I left the broadcast booth to manage the Padres, he called me before a game and said, "I don't want you to play Winfield today." I said, "Ray, I know how you feel, but we're playing the Dodgers, and they're fighting Cincinnati for the pennant. I have to play Winfield. He's my best player. If I don't play him, it'll look like we're giving up to the Dodgers."

He persisted. "I don't want you to play him," he said.

I played him anyway. Ray could have fired me, but he didn't. I don't know what his problem was with Dave Winfield. It might have been off-the-field stuff.

The Padres finally won a pennant in 1984, but Ray Kroc didn't live to see it. He died early in the year.

His wife, Joan, became the owner, and then Tom Werner, a show-business executive, took over with 14 minority partners. They called them the Gang of 15. That wasn't a fair thing because there were a lot of nice people in that group, but we didn't win with them.

Ray Kroc wasn't the only character around the Padres.

Ted Giannoulas became a celebrity as the San Diego Chicken, hired by a radio station. The Padres had a chicken mascot before him, but all that one did was walk around the aisles. Then Ted took over and put a little life into it, some showmanship. Once they hatched him out of a huge egg. He was a big part of the show at the Padres' old Jack Murphy Stadium, now called Qualcomm Stadium. And he had little chicklettes joining him. He did some crazy things, and the umpires helped out a little bit. He never talked, of course. That was part of his game plan. Now he does his routine at ballparks all over the country and, I presume, makes a lot of money.

There was also the Tuba Man, who was formerly a Marine lieutenant. He had a tuba and a group of seven or eight people who followed him around, prancing through the aisles. They were unofficial cheerleaders for the ballclub when we'd lose a hundred games every year.

The Friar is still here, and he has a girl partner, a female Friar, whom he works with on occasion. He rings the rally bell to get things going.

Now for the 1984 season.

The Padres won the National League West with ease, beating out Atlanta by 12 games, with Dick Williams in his third season as manager. We had Steve Garvey at first base, Alan Wiggins—who stole 70 bases—and Garry Templeton in the middle infield, and Graig Nettles at third base. Tony Gwynn led the league in batting at .351, and stole 33 bases. Our starting pitchers—Eric Show, Mark Thurmond, Ed Whitson, and Tim Lollar—weren't a memorable bunch, but they were good enough. And Goose Gossage won 10 games and had 25 saves.

We went to Chicago in the playoffs and lost the first two games. Then we beat the Cubs the next three in San Diego. Steve Garvey supplied the most dramatic moment in the Padres' history with his winning home run in Game 4. It was a fantastic moment. The whole atmosphere was charged. You can't imagine what it was like—the Padres in the World Series.

When Red Barber was broadcasting for the Brooklyn Dodgers, they said you could follow the games by just walking in the street. Everyone had their radios turned on. The action was coming through those open apartment windows. Well, you could have heard the play-by-play uninterrupted from Mexico to Santa Barbara when the Padres made it to the World Series. Every radio in San Diego was on the game.

Think of a laborer working his tush off from 7:00 in the morning to 4:00 in the afternoon every day. Baseball gives him an interest. I've always felt this is the greatest strength of baseball. People become part of the team and love it.

The Padres going to the World Series for the first time was tremendously exciting for me, and here in 1984 I wasn't even a player. It was 40-some years after my start in baseball, and I still felt a thrill.

When Garvey hit the home run, I said, "It's out of here. Padres win." And then I stopped. The crowd took over from there. That's all you needed. When the crowd is going bonkers, why try to talk over them?

But we got blistered by the Tigers in the 1984 World Series, losing in five games. What I remember most was what happened after the final game when the Padres tried to board their buses outside Tiger Stadium. A mob was out there.

There were two team buses, but we couldn't get on one of them because of the mob. It took almost an hour and a half before they got the police there to get us to the second bus so we could leave. Cars were burning in the distance. I was afraid they would start throwing things—rocks and stones. It was an incredible, dangerous scene, and I still can't understand it. Their team just won the World Series. Why were they getting mad at us? They should have been cheering us for letting them win, not that we weren't trying to beat them. That was the worst thing I've ever seen in sports.

In 1998 we went to the World Series again. Tony Gwynn and Ken Caminiti had great seasons, and Greg Vaughn hit 50 home runs. Kevin Brown, whom we got from the Marlins, pitched superbly, and Trevor Hoffman had become an ace reliever. But we were swept in the World Series by the Yankees.

After we lost Game 4 at Qualcomm Stadium before a record crowd of 65,427, the fans gave the players a 20-minute standing ovation, demanding that they come back on the field for a curtain call. "It was one of the most special moments in my life as an athlete," Trevor Hoffman said afterward. The fans had given him and his bullpen mates wild applause as they trudged off the field while the Yankees players piled on each other at the pitcher's mound.

All this after being swept.

Contrast that atmosphere with what happened in the Bronx. When we played the first two games at Yankee Stadium, the team buses were parked on the street up above the field. The players and the rest of the Padres' entourage weren't allowed to go the buses by themselves. They had to do it in groups of at least 10 with police protection.

When teams visit the big cities like New York, Chicago, and Philadelphia, it can be tough for them, and it can also be hard for players on the home teams there. When Ed Whitson was pitching for the Yankees, he couldn't even warm up. The fans at Yankee Stadium were booing him constantly. He had to leave. He just couldn't pitch there anymore. They literally ran him out of town. He had pitched well for the Padres before going to the Yankees, and then he came back to San Diego and had some good seasons.

The situation for Alex Rodriguez in New York has been difficult for him. Of course, he stopped some of those comments in 2007 with a bunch of home runs. But when he's struggling, I can hear the boos all the way from San Diego.

I don't recall many instances of the San Diego fans booing Padres players. The people here are totally different. Many are retired, and there's the military influence. They're used to taking directions and instruction. They don't do things like that. They have great empathy for the kids out here who are trying like hell and don't succeed all the time.

Not that Padres players never have complaints. Several of them were upset about the distance to the wall in right-center at Petco Park when it opened. The trouble is, the opposing team didn't have any trouble hitting them out of there. The ones who complained ought to have played in the old configuration at Yankee Stadium. They don't know what distance is. If you're in a ballpark, you play that park with your bat the way you should play it. You can't try to hit home runs over a wall 500 feet away. When the Dodgers played at the Coliseum their first seasons in Los Angeles, right-center field was way out there, but left field was short, so they had to put up a high screen. They said,

"There goes Duke Snider's bat." He couldn't pull the ball. But there was a guy, Wally Moon, also a left-handed batter, who hit the ball over the screen. His home runs were called "moon shots." He used the screen to his advantage.

Two Padres in particular are very special, so far as I'm concerned, for the way they are off the field. Everyone knows how great their careers have been. I'm talking about Tony Gwynn and Trevor Hoffman. Their character impresses me more than their skills as athletes. They're strong, they're conscientious, they give of themselves, they're not egotists. They're marvelous human beings.

Trevor is still going strong. They play the "Hells Bells" musical theme for him when he comes in from the bullpen, and the fans go crazy.

I attended the Hall of Fame induction ceremonies in July of '07 for Tony and Cal Ripken Jr. I walked into one tent on the Cooperstown grounds, and there were 700 people there from San Diego who had flown across the country to honor Tony. The Padres organization had a large representation, but these were just people who lived in San Diego and wanted to show their admiration. The weekend before that, the Padres honored Tony at Petco Park, and I spoke at that. I had him sign a Wheaties box with his likeness that they put on the market.

Tony still has a baseball presence in town. He's the coach of the San Diego State baseball team and he broadcasts some games on our local television channel. At one time ESPN wanted him full time, and he could be a top-flight analyst for them. He understands the game, he understands hitting beautifully. But he didn't want to spend his life traveling back and forth to the East Coast.

Tony is the most celebrated baseball player in any city anywhere. There was Williams in Boston, DiMaggio in New York, but nobody dominated the way Tony did in this town. And a great part of this is his character.

In terms of personal qualities, I'd like to relate something about John Moores, who has been the Padres' owner since late 1994.

My daughter Chelsea went to The Bishop's School in La Jolla, a very highly regarded private intermediate and high school. They were trying to get scholarships for about 20 percent of the kids—disadvantaged youngsters who are bright and need education. It costs about $25,000 a year to go to the school. The headmaster wanted to get a scholarship from John Moores. He asked me if I could help. John Moores went to The Bishop's School and had lunch with the headmaster and several other important people there, and I was with them. We walked around and we passed a dungeon that served as a workout room. The next day, John Moores wrote a check for $1 million and gave it to the headmaster to develop a new facility. And the name was "The Coleman Family Health and Fitness Center." I thought, "Oh my god, I can't do that." But Moores wouldn't think of it any other way. You ought to see that workout room—there's nothing in the country any better. That's the kind of person John Moores is.

After broadcasting half of the Padres' games on radio in 2006, I went back to a full schedule the following summer. I did one inning of play-by-play, the third, and I was the color analyst for the fourth, fifth, and sixth innings of each game. I also interviewed manager Bud Black before the games—what happened before and what's coming up. I've been doing those pregame interviews with Padres managers for more than 15 years.

In my early years in the Padres' broadcast booth, Rick Monday and Dave Campbell, both former major leaguers, of course, broke in with me. When he began broadcasting, Rick was not a conversationalist and he never asked me a question. I think he felt insecure since it was so new to him. He'd just focus on the game, head down. I feel that if you have a partner working with you, discuss the game with him. That's the idea. A guy like Johnny Bench, we would go back and forth while broadcasting together with CBS. He had his ideas of the game, and I had mine. We had a great time.

I still work with Ted Leitner, one of the best in the business. Ted has the brain of a scientist. He can tell you what's on page 368, third paragraph, of *Gone With the Wind*. He has a mind that remembers everything.

Here in San Diego we've been in only two World Series. I keep kidding the players that I deserve more than two in 35 years broadcasting for the Padres. I tell them, "Get moving."

The Man in the Dugout

"Maybe the players who turned away from me were right. I don't blame them. In fact, had I to do it all over again, I wouldn't have taken the managing job."

15

The Man in the Dugout

When the Padres' 1979 season was well along–the team a tailender as usual–Ray Kroc became fed up.

In late August, he was fined $100,000 by baseball commissioner Bowie Kuhn for tampering. He had told reporters he planned to invest between $5 million and $10 million in free agents and player development and had specifically mentioned the Yankees' Graig Nettles and the Reds' Joe Morgan as potential free agents he might pursue.

What was Kroc's reaction to the fine? He told the Associated Press in an interview that "Baseball can go to hell" and added, "There's a lot more future in hamburgers than baseball." He turned over control of the team to his son-in-law Ballard Smith, the executive vice president, though Ray remained as the owner. The Padres finished the season at 68-93.

I was friends with Bob Fontaine, the Padres' general manager. We grew up together, and then Bob signed with the Brooklyn Dodgers and pitched for their Pony League team in Olean, New York, when I was at Wellsville my first year in the minors. We used to sit and talk about the Padres and about management styles, and finally, sometime during the '79 season, Bob said, "Why don't you manage the club?"

"Good," I said. "I will if you're my pitching coach." I laughed it off and paid no attention to it. He said it a couple of times. Finally, toward the end of the year, I said, "Bob are you serious?" He said, "Yes."

Roger Craig, who had been a fine pitcher for the Dodgers in Brooklyn and Los Angeles, was still the manager. "What about Roger?" I asked. Fontaine said, "He's gone. We're not going to bring him back." I told him I'd think about it. My position was this: I had been broadcasting for the Padres for eight years. Except for one year, it was a desperate, awful time. Nobody could play well. I thought, *Oh god, anything would be better than this.* After broadcasting all these years of terrible baseball, maybe a change would be good.

We got down to a week or two before the season ended, and Bob said, "Are you going to manage the club?" I told him, "I'll take a shot. But if I take this job and it doesn't work, I want to come back as a broadcaster." He said, "Okay."

I'm sure Roger Craig was ticked off at losing his job. I'd be, too. Roger was a good manager.

Roger had taken the managing job in bizarre circumstances: he replaced Alvin Dark when Dark was fired during spring training in 1978. Roger managed the team to an 84–78 record, the first time the Padres had a winning season, and it seemed as if the franchise had finally gotten on the right track. But in '79 Rollie Fingers, the star reliever, hurt his elbow, and Ozzie Smith, who had been runner-up in the Rookie of the Year balloting the previous season, began the season in an 0-for-32 slump.

And so Roger Craig took the fall.

The Padres gave me a three-year, $200,000 contract just one season after Ballard Smith had said the team would never give a manager a multiyear agreement.

Fontaine told reporters that I believed in myself although I wasn't cocky. He said that his new manager had "been a success at everything he's ever undertaken in his life, even if he doesn't make a spiel about being Jerry Coleman."

I became the first person, as far as I know, who went from the broadcast booth to managing without ever having been a manager before.

Charlie Grimm, an outstanding first baseman in the 1920s and '30s, later broadcasted for the Cubs in between managing stints. He managed the Cubs for seven seasons in the 1930s, then went to the broadcast booth after Gabby Harnett replaced him. He was hired to manage the Cubs again in the 1940s, and he managed the Milwaukee Braves in the '50s.

Grimm had a third go-around as the Cubs' manager for part of the '60 season. Then he went to the broadcasting booth again, doing radio for WGN, in a trade of sorts for Lou Boudreau, who went from Cubs broadcaster to Cubs manager. Boudreau, of course, was a Hall of Fame shortstop and had been the player/manager for the Indians team that won the 1948 pennant.

Long after my stint as Padres manager, there were others who went from broadcaster to manager with no big-league experience in the dugout. Larry Dierker did it with the Houston Astros, Bob Brenly with Arizona, and Buck Martinez with the Toronto Blue Jays. But Brenly, a longtime catcher, who switched from the broadcast booth to the managing job with the Diamondbacks in 2001, had once been a bullpen coach for the Giants. Most of the better managers worked their way up. Willie Randolph had never been a manager before the Mets hired him, but he had been a coach with the Yankees for many years.

When Casey Stengel became the Yankees manager in 1949, it was almost 25 years since he had played in the major leagues, about the same time frame for my situation. But Stengel had been managing for years. The Yankees players knew that he had managed the Brooklyn Dodgers and the Boston Braves. They were bad teams, but that wasn't his fault. And he had managed in the minors after that, at Toledo and Oakland. Casey wasn't loved by the guys who had played for Joe McCarthy, like DiMaggio and Henrich and Rizzuto, and he had to deal with that. But he had some pretty darn good ballplayers and one of the greatest pitching staffs in history. And that made it easier for him.

So I told Bob Fontaine, "We're going to have a credibility problem here that we may not be able to overcome." I'd been out of uniform for more than two decades, and while I had been a broadcaster, that's looked at as another part of the game. You have the front office, you have playing personnel, and broadcasters are out there in left field. Ballplayers are used to being around their own. When they're not, they aren't comfortable. Guys coming out of the woodwork just aren't accepted. When you're off the field, removed from the game itself, players have a tendency to think, *Who is this guy? A broadcaster?* Some players thought I'd arrived from the moon. I was an outsider.

I'll leave the names of the players out. I'm not interested in casti-gating anybody, but there were some Padres players who never really accepted me as their manager. Three or four didn't like me—who I was or what I represented—right from the start. I wasn't surprised. Not that it changed where we finished, but when you have that, you don't get the full energy you need. And consequently it eventually arrested any chance we had. But we didn't have much of a ballclub, and we were up against Cincinnati and Los Angeles, powerhouse teams at the time.

Maybe the players who turned away from me were right. I don't blame them. In fact, had I to do it all over again, I wouldn't have taken the managing job. There was too much of a problem from the stand-point of "Who's this guy?"

It was hard to overcome that. Honestly, I don't recommend that for someone like me. No one knows who or what you are. You should go down and manage first in the minor leagues and learn your business. I never had a close relationship with my players. Stengel didn't have one with his, but he had a big edge in talent. You don't have to love people and be nice to them if you have talent. If you don't have talent, you have to coddle them along a little bit.

I did get an insight into the way players approached the game. Being a manager opened my eyes to the way modern-day players think compared to those in the years when I was a Yankee, when players had no control, no anything.

When I played, if you won, you got a bonus—a World Series check. And we kept the same basic units on the Yankees for years. We had the same four pitchers for four years, five years. Now you never see that. They're running off and getting better contracts someplace else. Today, if you have a pretty good year individually, you get a bonus in terms of your contract. The money is incredible. DiMaggio and Williams, Musial, Mantle, and Mays made $100,000 a year, which was good money then, but nothing compared with what you're talking about now.

When I played in New York, you either won or you lost. If you came in second, you lost. That was the Yankees' attitude. Today, you hit .250 and have 30 home runs, you get $6 million, maybe $8 mil-lion staring you in the face. And that, in a sense, is lifetime security.

Consequently, I found that many players wanted to do well but more for their own personal needs than winning the pennant. That's not as important as it was 50 years ago and before free agency. The motto for some modern players was: "I had my good year, I got the money." The team element at times is lost, and that's hurtful.

Early in my time managing the Padres, I remembered something that Gene Mauch, a scrappy infielder in his day, better known as a manager, once said to me. He told me, "The worst thing is the day that you realize you want to win more than the players do."

Any time you throw money out there, there's always less of a commitment to anything. That's the one thing that I do believe has changed the game dramatically. When you have players making 10 times more than the manager makes, they don't want to be led by this man, whoever he may be. I made $67,000 in my year as the Padres' manager.

And nothing beats money in terms of where a ballplayer is going to play. You can play in the hot tropics at 100 degrees every day, and if you pay them enough, they'll play there over a nice cool place on the East Coast somewhere. They have a thing here called the San Diego discount. Instead of getting $15 million, you get $12 million, or something like that, because it's a great place to play. Great climate. Very supportive fans. Players love to be here. But if you don't pay them, they're not going to play here. The San Diego situation may be a unique case, but basically for 99 percent of the people, if you're in baseball, or any sport for that matter, top dollar will win the job. Though if you get close to top dollar in San Diego, that might do it.

When I succeeded Roger Craig, the *Los Angeles Times* balanced my lack of managing experience with the fact I had played nine years for the Yankees, had won a Rookie of the Year Award in 1949, and had been named MVP of the 1950 World Series. It called me "a kind of emissary from the last true dynasty in baseball," noting that "in San Diego, which got its first major league franchise, the American Football League Chargers, in 1962, and wouldn't get the Padres for another seven years, this was tradition you don't find on the street."

At the news conference announcing my signing, I emphasized the team above the individual. "The only thing that counts is the unit," I said. "The only thing I did in baseball was play on championship teams. We came in fifth this year, and Dave Winfield could be the MVP. If Winfield hits .220 next year and we win, I'll be very happy. He won't be, but I will."

That said, I never talked to my Padres players about the Yankees of my day and the selflessness on those teams. It was too far removed. Nobody cares about the old days. It's not that important. It's now that counts.

In terms of my approach to managing, people wondered if I was using Casey Stengel as a model. "Everyone has been trying to pattern me after Casey," I told the *Los Angeles Times* during spring training. "I'm my own man now." But I added, "Whenever you play for someone, you obviously pick up some of his things. There's no way you can play for a Casey Stengel for 10 years and not pick up some ideas."

I did some things during the first few days of Padres spring training that were borrowed from Casey. He would instruct his players by walking with them from home plate to first base, to second base to third base. He'd cover all the problems and what you could do and couldn't do. "Okay, all you guys gather around," he'd say, and he'd take the players through each situation—two outs, one out, nobody on. Who can run, who can't. He'd cover all the contingencies that could occur at any time at that base.

Incidentally, the night before my hiring as manager was announced, another Coleman was running the Padres. Gary Coleman, the actor, was featured in the made-for-TV movie *The Kid From Left Field*, a remake of the 1953 Hollywood movie with Dan Dailey and Anne Bancroft. Gary's character, J.R. Cooper, was a batboy who manages the Padres to the World Series with the secret assistance of his father (played by Robert Guillaume), a baseball has-been working as a ballpark vendor.

The Padres' sportscaster in the Gary Coleman movie was yours truly. And Ed McMahon, who, as I've mentioned, had been a Marine pilot in Korea and helped smooth my way home after the armistice, also had a role in the picture. I took a lot of kidding about that film.

My Padres team started out at 22–19, and we were the talk of the baseball world. "Where did this come from?" We had some good pitching early on.

I even won an argument with an umpire, but by the time that dispute was resolved, I had been tossed out of the game. It happened in early May, during the second game of a Sunday doubleheader with the Mets at Shea Stadium.

In the second inning, Lanny Harris, the home-plate umpire, who had called two balks on Rollie Fingers the previous year, called one on our starting pitcher, Eric Rasmussen, for an illegal leg movement. When I came out to ask Harris about the call, he threw me out, citing a rule prohibiting a manager from protesting that type of balk call. Then the other three umpires came over, weighed in, and the balk call was reversed. My banishment wasn't.

The Mets scored three runs in the inning and we lost 6–2, but Rasmussen said afterward that he didn't feel badly. "All they were hitting were ground balls up the middle," he told the *Los Angeles Times*. "I'll admit this is kind of frustrating, but this kind of thing—not getting any offense—has been happening in my career for five years."

Rasmussen's career didn't get any brighter in 1980—he went 4–11. But he wasn't alone in his futility. After our good start, the pitchers started to falter, and then we went into a real nosedive. Bob Fontaine was fired shortly before the All-Star break and Jack McKeon, his assistant, replaced him as general manager. I called Ballard Smith, the Padres' president, and I said, "The guy who hired me just got fired and I'll step down if you want me to." And he said, "No, stay there."

Fontaine had been a Padres executive for 12 seasons and had outlasted five managers. But Smith said he was determined to make major changes if the club didn't shed its perennial losing ways. "I hope they all start worrying about their jobs," he told a news conference. "If they don't do better in the second half, we are going to clean house."

So I went to McKeon and I said, "Jack, here are the names of six players I want off this ballclub. They're a detriment more than they are a help. These guys can't help any club. They can't play baseball."

You might have heard the phrase "Trader Jack"—this is where McKeon got the name. Because, man, he had a free hand and he made a lot of moves. In the second half of the season, we played better. But it was too late. We had buried ourselves.

We had speed and pretty good defense, but we didn't have a lot of bats, and the pitching was way below par. That was the main problem. We set a record for stolen bases, the only time three men had stolen at least 50 for the same team. Ozzie Smith, Jerry Mumphrey, and Gene Richards did it. And we did have three future Hall of Famers—Dave Winfield in the outfield, Rollie Fingers relieving, and Ozzie, who was great at shortstop. When people pointed that out afterward, I would say, "Yeah, but what about the other 22 guys?" When you have only three or four people who can hit, and the rest are automatic outs, you don't have much going for you.

Our lineup went this way: Winfield, playing in right, didn't have a great year with us but he did okay. He got better after he left. Mumphrey, in center field, was good defensively and he might have had his best year when he played for me. He was a switch-hitter, great from the left side but weak from the right side. Gene Richards, in left field, was a fine hitter overall.

At first base, Willie Montanez was a happy-go-lucky guy but was tailing off. He had some good days and some bad days. But he was a quality ballplayer overall. Sometimes he lost his concentration, but to have it for all 162 games is very hard.

Ozzie Smith was brilliant at shortstop—as good as any shortstop who every lived—but he hit only .230 that year. He became a better hitter when he went to the Cardinals in a trade for Garry Templeton. His bat came alive. Part of that might have been the artificial turf in St. Louis. Balls got through the infield quicker.

Dave Cash at second base and Aurelio Rodriguez at third base were over the hill. Gene Tenace, our catcher, had that one big World Series with the Oakland A's. He was a better first baseman than a catcher.

As for the pitching, Randy Jones had been a 20-game winner twice for us a few years earlier and he won the National League's Cy Young Award in 1976. He was signed to a five-year, $2 million contract at the end of the '79 season. He started out the '80 season strong, including three consecutive shutouts, then came up with separated ribs pitching against Cincinnati on June 8 and aggravated the injury a few days later pitching at Philadelphia. He hurt his shoulder later on, never really pitched well after his good start, and wound up at 5–13. Rollie Fingers did a good job in relief. He went to the Milwaukee Brewers the next year and won the MVP Award as well as the Cy Young Award.

The rest of the starting pitchers didn't overwhelm anyone. Bob Shirley was okay. John Curtis did a pretty good job, but he was a number three or number four starter, maybe a number five. Steve Mura was okay but never developed into much of a pitcher. They paid Rick Wise a lot of money, but he never materialized into the pitcher they wanted him to be. John D'Acquisto, a San Diego kid, had been signed by the Giants to a nice bonus, had one good season with them, but never became the pitcher they hoped for. He wasn't with us either.

Overall, we were not a good ballclub. We were 73–89 and finished sixth, and last, in the National League West, two and a half games behind the fifth-place Giants. If you look at the numbers, we had the second-best record with the Padres ever up to then, except for Roger Craig two years before that. But I'm not patting myself on the back.

In the final week of the season I was told I wasn't coming back. It's devastating when you lose. You feel like you've failed. I was disappointed that I wasn't better, but it was a great experience. It opened my eyes to a lot of things. And, as agreed on when I took the job, I was able to go back to the broadcasting booth.

Managing is a crazy, stressful business. Look what happened with Mike Hargrove in Seattle in 2007. He got tired of managing and he just walked away even though the team was on a long winning streak.

I don't know how much the losing season contributed to this, but the following year I had my whole stomach redone. Chronic ulcer disease was what they called it. My stomach had always been sensitive and it particularly gave me fits after I came back from Korea. When they did the surgery, they cut a nerve, and it affected my digestive system. I had trouble for years, but I'm okay now.

Incidentally, I was given my coaches when I got the managing job. I didn't get to name them. As it turned out, I didn't get a chance to manage for a second year. If I had, I was going to have Frank Howard, Doug Rader, and a former catcher named Phil Roof as my coaches—all big guys. Frank went about 6'7" and 255 pounds. I was going to get three big bullies. I needed some big guys to grab certain players by the nape of the neck and talk to them seriously. Sometimes you need that kind of effect, and I needed it because I was small in stature and considered a wimp by most of the players.

Frank Howard replaced me as manager, but even with his physique he couldn't coerce the Padres into winning. He had a terrible time, and his 1981 team finished in a familiar spot—last in the NL West. And, like me, big Frank was gone as manager after a single season.

Life with Maggie

"We thought about the age difference.... But Jerry is such a high-energy person, I don't think I could have kept up with him if he had been any younger."

—Maggie Coleman

16

Life with Maggie

I've mentioned that in October 2006 Maggie and I celebrated our 25th wedding anniversary with a trip to my baseball past—Wellsville and Binghamton, New York, where I started out in the Yankees' farm system.

Maggie is a great lady—very beautiful, smart as a whip, and my ideal of what a woman should be. Marilyn Monroe—or the image of the dumb blonde—is at the bottom, and Deborah Kerr is at the top. And Maggie is a Deborah Kerr—a sophisticated, smart lady. We have a beautiful daughter, Chelsea, who is very, very bright and very charming. She's a senior at the University of Virginia and is planning to teach English in Japan when she graduates.

Maggie comes from a military family. Her father, Hardy Hay—a native of Waco known to his friends as Tex—is a retired Marine colonel and a combat veteran of three wars. He flew fighter planes in World War II, off Guadalcanal, the Russell Islands, Peleliu, and Okinawa, and shot down a Japanese fighter while protecting destroyers from kamikaze attacks. He flew a jet in the Korean War and a helicopter in the Vietnam War. When I retired from the Marine reserves, I was a lieutenant colonel. Since he's a retired full colonel, I tell people I have to salute him.

Maggie's mother, Frances Hay, a Bostonian, was a lawyer in the Marines when she met Tex at the old Mojave Marine air station in California when he was stationed there during World War II. She had graduated from Portia Law School for women in Boston. Harvard Law

School didn't admit women back then. They were married in 1945, and then Maggie's mom retired from the Marines.

I had known Maggie through her job for almost 10 years when we decided to marry. She had been obtaining donations from the Padres to fundraising auctions for the public TV station where she worked.

The life that I brought her into is not easy, especially when you're raising kids. Baseball people are gone all the time. You have to be a stable individual to survive that. And there was the age gap as well. I had just turned 57 and she was 31 when we married. How did this all work out? I'll let Maggie speak to that:

> Jerry and I were newly married when we saw *The Great Santini*. I'll never forget that movie—it was the story of my life.
>
> I was born in Long Beach, California, but I lived in a lot of places growing up in a Marine family. I mostly remember Tustin, California, near El Toro Marine Air Station. But we also lived outside of Paris for three years, and at Cherry Point, North Carolina, and then in Kansas City when my dad was completing his military career. I wound up going to four high schools—one in California, one in North Carolina, and two in Kansas City. I went on to the University of Kansas and graduated in 1971.
>
> I have a brother who is three years older than me and a sister who is almost eight years younger. I remember being in the backseat of our station wagon, and we'd entertain ourselves as we traveled from one end of the nation to the other. *The Great Santini* was our family story, down to the vehicle they were driving. And the dad getting the kids up at 3:00 or 4:00 in the morning so the family could get an early start, heading to the next assignment, the kids thrown in the backseat of the blue-and-white station wagon, grousing. The Santinis were going to South Carolina in one scene like that. We

were going to North Carolina. We were on the move every three years. It was the only life we knew.

It was as if our whole family was in the Marine Corps. Everything the family did reflected on the father, the Marine. There was a certain amount of pressure to behave right.

My mom didn't work when we were young, then resumed her career as a lawyer when we moved to Kansas City. She helped a consortium of small private colleges obtain government funding.

In 1972, after I had saved enough money, I drove myself from Kansas City to San Diego in my Volkswagen. My brother was in the navy and stationed in San Diego at the time. I fell in love with San Diego's natural beauty. Shortly after I arrived, I went to work for KPBS, the local public television station.

I organized the televised fundraising auctions, and that's how I met Jerry.

The Padres and Jerry had donated the chance to be Jerry's guest in the broadcast booth during a Padres game, with the bonus of being interviewed on the air during the visit. I escorted the woman who made the winning bid to the broadcast booth. Jerry and I immediately struck up a friendship based on our jobs. Because he was kind and outgoing, I started calling him to help me get donations from the Padres to sell on the air. Jerry would get me autographed bats and balls and would bring players to the auctions. Our relationship grew from there.

When we considered getting married, Jerry said, "I'll give you 10 years, and then I'll be too old for you," which is not a good way to start a marriage. It makes you a little nervous. He was 25 years older. But it didn't seem insurmountable. I wasn't a real kid anymore. I'd been supporting myself for 10 years. We thought about the age difference. It was there. You couldn't not think about it. But Jerry is such a high-energy person, I don't think I could have kept up with him if he had been any younger.

I'd never been married before. He, of course, had been married for quite a long time. You don't know what you're getting yourself into. You don't know what marriage is like until you're there. You just go—you jump. And that's the kind of person Jerry is.

I saw many fine qualities in Jerry. I admired his integrity. And he was such a solid person. He was reliable. He was there when I needed him in a way that no one had ever been for me. If I was going through something, he was supportive and understanding and not judgmental. He was fun. We had a similar sense of humor.

Considering that my father had been a Marine pilot in three wars, people might wonder whether Jerry's aerial combat in the Marines played a part in my being attracted to him. I don't think I knew much about that when we got married. At any rate, it's all way too Freudian to think about. I think you look for the qualities that a father has shown you are good qualities in a person. So probably that was there. I saw that and reacted to it. Jerry always made me feel safe, and that was a lot for me because growing up everywhere and nowhere, as I did, you don't feel like you belong anywhere. I felt at home with him and I could count on him. That's what I mean by his being reliable.

I have a lot of friends who talk about how they pictured their life being as an adult. I never had any pictures because our life was so funny growing up. There weren't people that we saw, there weren't marriages that we saw as kids, long term. There were Marine couples that my parents would bump into, but they would change. Since I didn't have any pictures in my mind, I figured that my life would be whatever I made it. I didn't have any preconceived notions about children, about a marriage, about anything.

Our daughter Chelsea was born in March 1985. Jerry brought us home from the hospital on a Friday and—I'll never forget this—departed the following day for the Padres' spring training camp in Arizona. I'm there with this baby, thinking, *Oh my god.* That was the way it went. In baseball, the women raise the children.

I'm very independent, but it was hard. It was lonely. I envied people who had husbands with more reliable schedules who would be romping on the beach with their kids on weekends, because we didn't have that. When you think about the seasons you don't have in baseball, it's summer. It's the end of February through October sometimes. It's many of those family vacation times, Fourth of July, the picnics. That was the hardest thing—not being able to do things as a family during the summer.

Our wedding was a good example of the way our life has had to accommodate baseball. We scheduled the ceremony for October 5, a Monday, and made it for late afternoon. We were working it around the baseball season. But Jerry was going to do the playoffs for CBS. He missed our rehearsal dinner Sunday evening because he got home late. He left town at 6:30 the morning after our wedding to fly to Montreal and broadcast the Expos-Dodgers playoff series. I went back to work and, five days later, joined him in Montreal.

So my honeymoon with Jerry included Jack Buck and the rest of the CBS radio crew. After we finished the playoffs, we traveled to New York, then on to France for our real honeymoon.

My childhood probably helped me prepare for being the wife of a man in baseball. My father had been gone a lot when I was young. My mother was the only one there much of the time. I remember what it was like when my dad was away for a year in Vietnam.

Being alone while your husband was away didn't seem bizarre to me. Over the years, we've seen the young wives of some players struggle when their husbands are out of town to the point of crying. They can't cope. I never quite understood that. You do what you have to do. But they didn't.

In terms of baseball, I'm a casual fan—but far more of a fan than I would have been had I not married into the sport. My grandmother in Boston was a big baseball fan, so it was part of the conversation in our house. My older brother was always a huge baseball fan, and I used to go to games with him.

My passion is art. I used to drag Jerry to all these art openings and museums. And he would act like he cared.

When Chelsea was young, I didn't have any friends with young children. I had been working. I had a different kind of life. Luckily, I met a woman, Anne Halsey-Smith, who has been a good friend. She is the granddaughter of Admiral Bull Halsey. We're the same age. Our kids are two weeks apart. And Anne's husband is a ship's captain, meaning she also was on her own a lot.

Anne grew up here in La Jolla, so she knew people. That was how I started meeting other women with young children. And La Jolla is like a little village. Chelsea went to a preschool in La Jolla and still has friends from those early school days. You know people in the bookstore and the grocery store. Chelsea grew up in one house. I don't even know the locations of all the houses where I was raised.

I'm committed to a lot of volunteer work with the emphasis on education. I was on the board at The Bishop's School in La Jolla when Chelsea was a student there, and I was the board president two years after she graduated. I also helped start a foundation to support Garfield High—an alternative public high school in San Diego for at-risk kids.

I am also involved in Las Patronas—"the patronesses"—which is a group for La Jolla women that has been serving the community since World War II. They hold an annual ball on the tennis courts of the La Jolla Beach and Tennis Club for a variety of charities. Las Patronas distributes about $1.5 million a year to charity. I'm proud to say I am a past president of Las Patronas and remain an adviser.

When I worked with Las Patronas, not many of the women's husbands traveled like Jerry did, but they were doctors, lawyers, very successful in their own right, and they all worked their tails off. They all traveled some. So it wasn't as if I thought that I was so burdened because my husband was gone all the time working. But the hard part was that their husbands could be there if it was a special occasion or a wedding or a Fourth of July party, but Jerry couldn't. He didn't have any flexibility. I went to this ball without him several times because he couldn't be there. People knew that Jerry was going to be gone during certain times of the year. He couldn't just take a night off. Of course, it's the only married life I've ever known.

When we were first married, and for a number of years, Jerry worked three jobs for the Padres, so he was busy during the winters as well. In addition to broadcasting TV and radio, he was the team's director of broadcasting and became involved in development of cable TV outlets. He had to attend winter meetings around the country to meet with other broadcasting directors.

Jerry adores Chelsea and she adores him. When she was a baby and we'd be out with her in her stroller at a shopping center, people would come and say, "Oh, so this is Chelsea," because they recognized Jerry, and he used to talk about her on the air all the time. Growing up in this town, which was smaller when she was a kid, she thought everybody knew who she was. She didn't know it was different for other kids.

I don't believe there were a lot of difficulties for Chelsea in being the daughter of a local celebrity. But I think sometimes she would have liked to have been anonymous and not have people have certain expectations of her. When she went to college, she was really trying to be just Chelsea Coleman, not Chelsea Coleman, daughter of Jerry Coleman.

Her second year out of high school, she took a year off and went to culinary school in Italy. We went to visit her. On the street in Florence, we ran into someone she knew from her culinary school. She introduced us, and as we walked away she said, "He's from New York and he's a huge Yankees fan." I said, "Oh, does he know Jerry's connection?" She looked at me very pointedly and said, "No, no one does." It was clear that she was just being herself and no other identity. No assumptions.

There was a certain lack of privacy for us as a family. What's hard is having Jerry's attention because when you're out, Jerry is so conscious of being courteous to people that they approach him all the time. You can be out to dinner, you can be trying to have a conversation, and there are five people involved in your conversation. His style on the air locally is so friendly that people feel they know him, that they're on a personal basis with him. No one hesitates to speak to him. You're aware of when people are staring or when they try to eavesdrop.

During the winters, we have time to get away. Some time back, we tried skiing as a family. Chelsea started to ski at age five, and I had taken lessons. Every January she and I would go to Vail. Then Jerry insisted he was going to try. It scared me to death because natural athletes, which Jerry definitely is, think they can do anything. But he couldn't ski; I was pretty sure he was going to kill himself and take a few people with him, and I tried to dissuade him from going on the slopes, which he eventually did do. I finally gave up on skiing because I fell really bad and I got scared. So Jerry and I decided we would go snowshoeing.

We went to Beaver Creek, Colorado, and I remember one day in particular. It's very hard going—you're at altitude—but he was outpacing me. He was 20 feet ahead, and I was chugging along, and then I looked up and he was gone. It was a gray day, the visibility poor, but still, there was no place for him to go. Where'd he go? And then I found him. He had stepped off the trail just a shade and got in up to his chest. I was laughing so hard I couldn't help him. But he wasn't thinking it was that funny. He finally just had to climb out, but that's hard to do when you're in soft snow. So that was the end of our winter sports. By now, Chelsea is old enough to go on her own and go with friends.

Jerry keeps fit by walking in the La Jolla hills. He walks five miles every morning with our German shepherd, Gus. Jerry likes to say, "I don't know if I'm walking Gus or he's walking me." They're both in great shape.

Then and Now

"After more than six decades in baseball, as a player, executive, manager, and broadcaster, the game still has a pull, it's still exciting. I love being at the ballpark."

17

Then and Now

To this day, I never say, "Oh boy, I had a great time," or "Oh boy, how did that go wrong?" I say, "Okay, what's next?" And I'm sincere about that. What's up front interests me. What's behind me doesn't interest me. It's over—it's done. I'm not somebody who dwells on the past at all.

But in reflecting, I continue to feel that my military service was the most important thing I've ever done.

In June 2000, the 50th anniversary of the start of the Korean War, Major League Baseball asked me to attend a wreath-laying ceremony at the Tomb of the Unknown Soldier in Arlington National Cemetery. I'd never visited Arlington before. I'd never even been to the Iwo Jima Memorial just down the road. I'm not a tourist by nature. But driving through Arlington, with its thousands of gravestones, it was incredible. You can't not be awed.

The chairman of the Joint Chiefs of Staff, General Henry Shelton, and the baseball commissioner, Bud Selig, were at the ceremony. And so was a man unknown to the public—Robert Neighbors Jr., the son of Bob Neighbors, who had played shortstop for the St. Louis Browns. His father was a major in the air force and had flown a B-26 bomber in the Korean War. On August 8, 1952, he went out on a mission and never returned. Bob Neighbors was the only major leaguer killed in the Korean War, one of 8,100 Americans still unaccounted for.

That ceremony at Arlington was one of the highlights of my life. I told people for the first time then what the Marines mean to me— loyalty and responsibility to others before considering yourself. I said that the most important thing in my life was not what I did in baseball, but what I did in the service of the Marines during two wars—five years on active duty.

What you have in the Marines is a closeness. If you're flying and you hear a Mayday, as I did when Ted Williams was trying to get back to base with a shot-up plane, that's your brother. That's you. The Marine Corps brings you into a situation where you become less important than the whole. The things that really count are part of the unit. There are so many Marine heroes who have given their lives for their friends.

In World War II I was a patriot, and I was 18—the minimum age—when I entered the navy's pre-flight program. I wanted to get into the war. I was afraid the war would end before I got there. The second time around, when I was called up for Korea, I was 27 years old, and I wasn't quite as anxious. But I never regretted the fact that I went into the service in my second trip, although it took away most of the prime of my baseball career. That's pretty insignificant, considering what went on in the world.

For years after World War II I'd get letters from my fellow pilots, and I've kept in touch to this day with one of them, Bob Means, who shared a tent with me and a couple of other fliers in the Philippines. Now he walks with a cane and speaks softly.

Several years ago I received a letter from Brian Meenan, a son of Patrick Meenan—or Stretch, as I called him—my gunner in that Dauntless dive-bomber during World War II. Stretch was seriously ill. I gave him a phone call and we talked about our times together.

He had become a New York City police officer after the war, lived in the Kingsbridge section of the Bronx, near Yankee Stadium, and he and his wife, Julia, raised five children. Occasionally, he took the kids to Yankee Stadium. Brian Meenan has a flying career of his own. He's a graduate of the Air Force Academy, a brigadier general in the Air Force Reserve, and a pilot for Continental Airlines.

A while back, Stretch's daughter, Patricia Lapierre, was out in San Diego with her 11-year-old son, Tom. I was their host for four Padres games. I had Tom sit next to me in the broadcast booth with a headset on, listening to my call of the game, and he kept score along with me. I got Brian Giles to autograph a bat for him.

We have a little magazine for VMSB-341, my World War II squadron. But I don't see many references to pilots from the Pacific war. Most are probably dead. My generation is slowly sliding out.

After the war, I had another chance to meet Joe Foss, the Marine ace who won the Medal of Honor for his exploits off Guadalcanal in 1942. It was the first time I had seen him since he spoke to our training group at St. Mary's Pre-Flight after he had been called home to receive the Medal of Honor from President Roosevelt.

People forget—and some don't know history. In the months after 9/11, Foss had the Medal of Honor in his jacket when he was trying to pass through security at the Phoenix airport. He was en route to West Point for a speech and thought the cadets would like to see what the medal looks like. The airport security people told him he couldn't take it aboard the plane because it could be used as a weapon of some sort. He told them how he had been given the medal by FDR, but that made no impression, since the guards didn't know what the Medal of Honor was. Who were these people who knew nothing about the country? Well, finally, they let him on the plane.

I remained in the reserves until 1964, when I retired as a lieutenant colonel. I do some promotional work for the Marine Corps. I've tried to help out with the Flying Leatherneck Historical Foundation and Aviation Museum at Miramar. They have a new Marine museum at Quantico that's stunning. I contribute to that. November 10 is the Marine Corps's birthday. I do what I can to publicize that, although if I went to everything I was invited to, I'd have to stop living. At the aerospace museum in the center of San Diego, they have a Dauntless dive-bomber, the type of plane I flew in the Solomons and the Philippines.

They call the Padres the team of the military. They give all kinds of things to active duty military and retired, and they've had games where the players wear military camouflage as a salute to the armed forces. You have the naval base in San Diego—there are two or three aircraft carriers in port all the time—along with the Marines' Camp Pendleton a few miles off and a huge Coast Guard base. I think there are hundreds of thousands of military and retired military in this area.

In 2007, the Padres had an intriguing guy working out at their spring camp in Arizona—a Marine named Cooper Brannan who had lost the pinky on his left hand in Iraq in a grenade explosion. He had pitched in high school and once dreamed of being a major leaguer. But he enlisted in the Marines after 9/11. A friend of his had told Sandy Alderson, our chief executive officer and a former Marine officer, about Brannan during ceremonies for the 231st anniversary of the Marine Corps in November 2006. Sandy invited him to work out with the Padres, and he remained at our spring base in Arizona for extended spring training when our season started. He's a right-hander. He regained use of his left hand after several operations and physical rehabilitation. He's a good-looking kid. I think if he can learn to pitch, he'll be able to overcome his injury.

As for keeping in touch with my old buddies in baseball, I've gone to a few old-timers' games at Yankee Stadium. My broadcasting work kept me away most of the time. In 2007 I was there when they were honoring the Yankees' 1977 World Series championship team. Most of the guys were 20 or 30 years younger than me, and I knew them mainly by their reputation.

I spent much of that weekend with Bobby Brown, my boyhood pal from the San Francisco sandlots, my Yankees teammate, and fellow Korean War veteran. We were the two oldest former Yankees introduced that day. I turned 83 on September 14, 2007, and Bobby reached 83 on October 25. Yogi will be 83 in the spring of '08.

Bobby, Yogi, Charlie Silvera, and I are the only surviving Yankees who played on all the World Series championship teams from 1949 to 1953. When we were kids, Bobby and I played for the Sherry Liquors team, a semipro club, in the San Francisco area. Charlie and I played on the same team when we were 10 years old and we were teammates at Wellsville in the Pony League in '42. Bobby had gone to Galileo High School, Charlie to St. Ignatius, and I had been at Lowell—all in San Francisco. Imagine the odds of three boyhood friends winding up as teammates on five straight championship teams.

The autograph-seekers were all over the place at that old-timers' weekend. All the invitees were staying at a Sheraton on Seventh Avenue, and you couldn't get from one side of the lobby to the other without being asked to sign. Some of the people had it all organized into books—"Sign on Page 12" or something like that.

DiMaggio used to be the kingpin for years at old-timers' day, then Mantle was the guy. Now Yogi or Whitey Ford are the top stars. But at this event, Bobby Murcer, battling brain cancer, supplied the emotional highlight. I was broadcasting for the Yankees when Bobby came up. I remember that he wanted to go to some great Broadway play. I happened to know the guy who was the producer, so I got two tickets for him. He never forgot that. Bobby had been heralded as the next superstar, the next Mickey Mantle. They both came from Oklahoma, of course. Bobby was a good player but he really didn't hit his stride until he was traded to the San Francisco Giants. Basically, it was unfair to place that burden on him.

I didn't play in the old-timers' game at the Stadium—it was exactly 50 years since I was last wearing pinstripes—but the next day I was in left field for an inning at the ballpark on Staten Island, where the Yankees have a Class A team. That was a three-inning game featuring some of the old-timers who had been at Yankee Stadium on Saturday, and we shook hands with the fans. I was thinking, *God, don't let someone hit anything to me.* Nobody did. If a ball came out there, I'd have stopped it with my foot. A few guys, the younger old-timers, hit most of the time, and the fans loved it. The ballpark is spectacular. You could look out and see the Statue of Liberty and the harbor, even the Empire State Building. It's quite a contrast to Ruppert Stadium, the old ballpark where I played for the Newark Bears in 1948.

In thinking back to the Yankees of my era, I remember the last time I saw Casey Stengel. He was retired in the Los Angeles area and I was doing a broadcast for the Padres late in the 1975 season. I had to get pregame stuff, and he wanted to talk, and I knew it, but I couldn't speak with him because I simply didn't have the time. I said, "Casey, I've got to go." He said okay. I have the feeling in reflection that he knew more about what was going on with him physically than others did. I was the only one on the field that day who was one of his guys. I was there during his greatest heyday—the five straight World Series championships. And I was there as a broadcaster when the Yankees kept winning. Casey was dead a few weeks after that brief visit. I regret that I wasn't able to speak with him that day at the ballpark.

In looking at baseball today in comparison with my Yankees years, I'll say this first: every player thinks his baseball generation was the greatest one. Frankie Frisch, the Hall of Famer and a good friend of mine, would boast of his era in comparison with "you guys," meaning his successors, who couldn't quite cut it, as he saw things.

I don't look at it that way. The guys today, they're enormous. And they're better. They're bigger, faster, stronger than ballplayers ever were. I don't say they're smarter, but these kids today are great athletes. If you take some of the superstars of 50, 60 years ago, they wouldn't even make some teams. Can you imagine someone like a Phil Rizzuto or a Luis Aparicio, both Hall of Fame shortstops, going up against Derek Jeter? They couldn't hit with him. And hitting is the dominant factor in baseball.

When you walk into Yankee Stadium and you look at Jeter and Alex Rodriguez, they're both 6'3", and these are infielders. Rizzuto was 5'6", and George Stirnweiss was 5'8". I was 5'11" and I only weighed 160 pounds. Billy Johnson was 5'10". The guys in my day were a bunch of midgets by comparison. Johnny Mize, the first baseman for the Cardinals and then my teammate on the Yankees, was 6'2" and about 215 pounds. He was maybe the biggest man in baseball at the time. Now they've got 60, 70, or more in the majors like that and bigger.

And today's guys don't play the same game as we did. It's a power game. The home run has become dominant so they don't know about hit-and-run and bunts. That was a game that I played. The game today is, how far can you hit the ball? I've seen the pitcher walk the first two batters on eight pitches, and the next guy came up and swung at the first pitch and popped up. That's not working the pitcher. Those kinds of things happen endlessly. The home run defines the game today—it's fan appeal and money. If you hit 25 home runs and bat .250, you get

$8 million. If you hit five home runs and bat .250, you get $2 million or maybe not that much.

Earl Weaver said the greatest thing in baseball is a three-run home run. Yeah, that's true—if you can hit one. But there are guys trying to hit the ball over the wall who can't do it. And they don't know how to work a pitcher.

The pitching is tougher nowadays. It's harder to hit now than it was in the 1940s and '50s. We'd have four starters and maybe a spot starter, and the other guys—go to the bullpen and if we need you, we'll call you. The old story of 50, 60 years ago was: "Hey, make that guy work. It's a hot day. We'll get him in the fifth and sixth inning." Today, you don't see him anyway because there's another guy coming in that maybe pitches better than the first guy does. Now you have starters, middle relief, setup, closers. You're liable to see three, four pitchers unless the starter has a great day. And these guys who come in from the bullpen are throwing 95 miles an hour. The pitchers are better, bigger, stronger.

But the thing that amazes me are the arm problems that are rampant, all over baseball—the Tommy John surgery and the like. Raschi, Reynolds, Lopat, Ford, and Byrne never had a serious arm problem that I can recall. Lemon, Feller, Wynn, and Garcia with the Indians and Trucks, Trout, and Newhouser with the Tigers never did either, as I remember it. Maybe they're building too much muscle today.

In the field, it's a one-handed game. I would last maybe five days as an instructor today because we were told to go the ball, make it hit you in the chest. Don't reach for the ball, go for it. Move back and forth. We were taught to catch the ball with two hands. If you do that, you've got it right. And yet I see plays that several second basemen and short-stops make that we never made. They've got great gloves. My mentor, Frank Crosetti, as I've said, had a glove that looked like a motorman's. He had to catch the ball with two hands. Today you don't have to. The players have great gloves and they have great reactions.

In terms of work ethic, things are different. Nobody in my era ever told the manager he was hurt. There was a guy behind you looking to take your job, and you needed the money. These guys today probably make as much in meal money as I did in salary in my first year. I got all the way up to $18,500 eventually. The way the Yankees sold their contract to you was, *Look, you're going to be in the World Series.* We were in the World Series every year, so you had to accept that as gospel. But that wasn't a salary. That was just a bonus.

These guys today have a groin pull here, a charley horse there, a rib-cage bruise here, and it's only June. Pick up the papers, they've got five guys every day who can't pitch anymore, can't run anymore. In 1950, which became my best year, I was going to conserve my strength for the season, so I didn't do a lot of work in the spring, a lot of running. I got a minor charley horse, and I was taped from knee to groin on both legs for six weeks, but I ran and I never took a day off unless they made me take one. I was lucky in terms of serious injury. I got beaned twice, once in the minors and once in the major leagues. The only really bad injury I had was that shattered shoulder in 1955.

And in today's game, forget about that hard-nosed stuff when it comes to relating to opposing players. If you go to the ballpark early, you see both teams in the field, and the players are chatting and hugging the guys on the other team. Free agency brought that about. You have guys who played with five, six clubs, and they meet former teammates all the time. The way you looked at it in my day, the customer would wonder, "Who's that guy talking to? That's the enemy." I never spoke to an opposing player in my life except for Mickey Vernon, the Washington Senators' first baseman, and Bobby Doerr, the Red Sox second baseman. That was it. Mickey was a good guy, Bobby was a good guy. When I was playing, if you were caught talking to an opposing player, you were fined $50 by the league. One umpire was in the stands during batting practice to look for fraternization.

It's a totally different world now—it's not worse, just different.

One big difference involves teaching the game. We had three coaches—Bill Dickey at first base, Frank Crosetti at third base, and Jim Turner, the pitching coach. Now teams have eight coaches. They're all over the place. A bullpen coach is probably pretty valuable. If you're calling down to the bullpen, for example, to "get Jones up," you want to know if "he's not doing too well today" and maybe he can't get anybody out. Other than that, I don't know that all those extra people giving advice really helps.

Beyond the uniformed coaches, there's been a debate going on for a while on how to build a ballclub—whether to be guided by computers, by statistical analysis. Much of this statistical stuff bears out, but you can't put a guy's heart, his guts, his intelligence on a computer. You can say, *Well, he drove in a lot of runs in A ball, C ball, D ball, and high school, college, and so forth.* It doesn't necessarily mean it's going to work in the big leagues. There's a balance that has to be met. I want to know how a guy reacts in certain situations. I have a pet thing. Someone might say, "This guy was 8-for-17 off Joe Jones." I say, "Yeah, that was then, this is now." Things change rapidly in baseball.

If you're going to sit and computerize everything, you're not going to make it work. There are too many intangibles involved that make a great ballplayer. Is a guy a winning player? And when does he get a hit? Does it win a game? You could be ahead 10-2 and hit a home run; what does that mean? A computer might send a flag up—hey, let's look at this guy. Look at these numbers here. And then you go out and see what else he has.

As for scouts, do you want the guys with modest experience who can analyze statistics and work with computers or do you look to the "lifers" who to a large degree might rely on instinct and the fruit of all those years knocking around ballparks? Incidentally, it takes years to find out if a scout knows what he's doing. He's going to give you recommendations on players, and finally, about the third or fourth year, you say, "This guy's been wrong all the time," or, "This guy's never missed," or, "He's half right and he's half wrong."

That being said, it's clear that everything in baseball has been upgraded immensely from the 1940s and '50s. The conditions are far better—the stadiums, the clubhouses, the fields themselves. You look at all the new ballparks—they're spectacular cathedrals. And attendance is up. There's nothing wrong with baseball today; in fact, it's getting better.

Baseball has something going for it that other sports do not. Everybody in the United States has stood up at home plate—boy or girl—and swung at a baseball, or a substitute for a hardball, at some point. They've had a bat in their hands or a broomstick. Maybe they've hit a tennis ball or a softball. Not many people that I know have shoulder pads and run into each other in football. So they know how hard baseball is. That's what makes the game great. And many people don't like the job they have. They're just working to get by, support their families. The baseball team, its fortunes played out daily over a long season, the stuff of arguments, gives people an identity, it becomes part of their lives. They're still mad in Brooklyn 50 years later because they took the team away from them.

Clubs make a very strong effort to get out and help disadvantaged kids, at the same time hoping to keep them as fans when they grow up. Some players invite groups of kids to the ballpark every Saturday. The players spend their own money. They make a lot, so they can afford to do it, but that's really good. The Knothole Gang doesn't exist anymore, as it did in Brooklyn with Happy Felton's pregame show, but every now and then you'll hear about efforts with the kids. Dave Winfield, a Padres executive now and a Hall of Famer, often has large groups of kids as his guests, as do Padres players. It's important to give them a chance to not only see baseball but to live a little bit.

And baseball has become an international game. They're setting up camps in the Dominican Republic and Venezuela and so forth to train these players. You've got Japanese, Koreans, Australians. The Padres' Sandy Alderson has gone to China a couple of times to see what's going on. Someday you'll find scouts from other countries coming over here.

Players in Latin America can see what's happening. It was the same thing during the Depression years, where everybody went to play baseball because they didn't want to stand in bread lines. I'll bet you a great percentage of the players in the '30s and in the early '40s were Depression kids who had no money. They were dead broke, so they went to play baseball to make $75 a month instead of getting nothing just walking around.

What you do need are a few marquee players who are also figures of adulation. There are great players out there like young Ryan Howard in Philadelphia, Prince Fielder in Milwaukee, and Albert Pujols in

St. Louis who are outstanding image-makers for baseball. You must train today's players—what they represent and who they are. That is a challenge because a lot of them get the money and get into themselves and they go crazy.

I've said that the two greatest Padres—Tony Gwynn and Trevor Hoffman—are admirable figures for me, not simply for their deeds on the field but for their strength of character.

That brings me to the issue of steroids. Baseball must clear this up. They've got to get it straightened out. Winning is considered the most important thing in sports. But winning fairly is more important to me. The steroid situation is one of the most inappropriate things I can think of. It's not the same thing as seeing if some guy is throwing a spitter. It's dramatically cheating.

Baseball lives on its records. If all the suspicions are confirmed, steroids are the one thing that has affected the most significant records dramatically. You can see some guys—20 home runs, then 50 home runs, 60 home runs, and then they're down to 20 again. You say, "Ah, something's wrong there." Things like that have happened with a lot of players.

It wasn't illegal, but we know that Mark McGwire took andro, a supplement. When he testified before Congress, he wouldn't say whether he took steroids. He hurt himself tragically with that appearance. It was sad. He looked so bad instead of facing up to it. I saw Mark from the time he was a rookie until he finished. I used to interview him. He looked like a giant redwood at the end.

The specter of steroids has cast a dark shadow over the game. Every record-setting performance or milestone achievement raises doubts and casts suspicion—even when it shouldn't. But it happens because steroids have been part of baseball. No one can deny that. And the investigations belatedly undertaken by baseball will surely result in further revelations. What is unclear is how long the dark cloud of steroids will linger over the game.

Will the game's hallowed records ever be held in such high esteem again? Or will every achievement be questioned? Are 500 homers in this era as meaningful as 500 homers were less than a generation ago? Public opinion currently says no.

Players are naturally bigger and stronger than they were 40 years ago. As I've stated before, conditioning programs are light-years ahead of where they were when I played. But some of the power numbers we've seen recently defy natural physiological progression. *Performance-enhancing drugs* was not a term I heard until the 1990s. Now it seems to pop up daily across the sports spectrum to the detriment of everyone.

Baseball and its fans have been victimized. The biggest disservice has been to the players who have remained clean. Their peers who used steroids pulled them into the abyss simply through association.

It may be that the kids who are getting caught are mostly minor leaguers and ignorant. But today anyone who takes steroids is insane. And baseball still has no way of understanding what has happened with human growth hormones. That's still out there.

It looks pretty damaging, but these issues remain to be played out in court and through investigations, or perhaps voluntary admissions. I have no proof or personal interest in this. But for me, Roger Maris's one-year home-run record and Hank Aaron's career homer record still stand in the sense that they are truly untainted.

And the suspicions go beyond the power hitters. I was discussing steroids with a player I respect who said, "It's the pitchers." That's all he said. My jaw opened up. Everybody looks at the home runs—you think about Bonds, McGwire, Sosa, Rafael Palmeiro—but you never think about the pitchers. How many of them have used steroids? Who knows?

I think that the players' union, which has really controlled baseball, created the steroid problem. They hid things that should have been exposed years ago. I'm for the union, but I think that was one terrible mistake the leaders made. They should have directed their attention to this immediately, stopped it on the spot, and we wouldn't have this problem we have now.

The penalties aren't strong enough now. My proposal: the first time you're caught, it's a 100-day ban, and the second time, one year. The third time, you're gone.

∞ • ∞

As for my life in the public eye beyond the ballpark, I do what I can to honor and promote the Marines. I'm in the Marine Corps Sports Hall of Fame at Quantico, Virginia. I was inducted in 2005 together with my fellow Marine veterans Elroy "Crazy Legs" Hirsch, a football star at Wisconsin and Michigan and with the Los Angeles Rams; Paul Arizin, the Hall of Fame basketball player with the Philadelphia Warriors; and Butch Keaser, an Olympic wrestler.

In addition to the Marines' sports hall, I'm in the National Radio Hall of Fame, the San Diego Padres Hall of Fame, and the Bay Area Sports Hall of Fame. I get about 50 letters a week, mostly for autographs. If you hang around long enough, maybe something good happens.

My career in pro baseball goes back to 1942, that season with the Wellsville Yankees at age 17, and I'm entering my 45th year as a base-ball broadcaster—first with the Yankees, then CBS, and now with the Padres. After more than six decades in baseball as a player, executive, manager, and broadcaster, the game still has a pull, it's still exciting. I love being at the ballpark. Every day is a different game and different things happen. I see things every now and then that I'd never seen before.

Baseball is the hardest of all sports—no question about it. When you want to define the difference between baseball and any other sport, it comes down to hitting a ball. You can have great athletes like Michael Jordan—he went to Double A and hit .150. If you can't hit a baseball, you can't play. And hitting it is the single most difficult thing in sports. A golfer has great touch, except that the ball is standing still. If you're standing at home plate with a guy throwing the ball 100 miles an hour, there's a fear factor in your mind. You might get hit in the head.

In July 2005 I was inducted into the broadcasters' wing of the Baseball Hall of Fame in Cooperstown as the recipient of the Ford C. Frick Award for major contributions to baseball broadcasting, named for the former baseball commissioner and National League president who had once been a sportswriter and a broadcaster. The voters for the award, presented annually since 1978, were the 14 living recipients and six broadcast historians. It was so gratifying that my peers put me there—my fellow broadcasters brought me in.

227

When it comes to speeches, I don't get too emotional. The thing I worry about is, what am I going to say? I always feel that less is better than more. The greatest speech in history is the Gettysburg Address—and it's one of the shortest. I had the shortest speech of those being inducted—the others were Wade Boggs and Ryne Sandberg as players and Peter Gammons in the writers' wing. I didn't read my speech. I tried to remember what I wanted to say.

I introduced my wife, Maggie; my daughters, Diane and Chelsea; my granddaughter, Courtney; my grandson, Christopher; and other family members. I thanked John Moores, who kept the Padres in San Diego, and I said thank you to Bobby Brown, my oldest friend in baseball, and to Yogi Berra and Whitey Ford, for being there. I paid tribute to Phil Rizzuto, my teammate and broadcast partner, who, at age 87, couldn't make the trip and passed away shortly thereafter. I related some light-hearted remembrances.

And I told the crowd, "I've done clinics throughout Europe. I was in Japan and in Canada and Mexico broadcasting games. I played exhibition games throughout Japan, Okinawa, in the Philippines, on Guam, in the Hawaiian Islands. I made a trip to Vietnam for baseball. And I have broadcast and been in just about every small village and major city in the United States. But today, on this golden day here in Cooperstown, a journey that started 63 years ago, I feel that finally, finally, I've come home."

Notes

Newspapers

The Dallas Morning News, Los Angeles Times, New York Herald Tribune, New York Post, The New York Times, New York World-Telegram and Sun, North County (Calif.) News, The San Diego Union-Tribune, San Francisco Chronicle.

Books, Articles and Monographs

Allison, Fred H. "Marine Air Support." *Marine Corps Gazette*, Nov. 1, 2006.

Barber, Red. *Rhubarb in the Catbird Seat.* New York: Doubleday, 1980.

Chapin, John C. "And a Few Marines: Marines in the Liberation of the Philippines." History and Museums Divisions, Headquarters, United States Marine Corps, 1995.

Coleman, Jerry. Press Conference, National Baseball Hall of Fame, July 30, 2005.

Department of Defense. "Brief History of the Marine Corps in the Korean War," 2000.

Fanton, Ben. "How It Was in the Old Days of Class 'D' Baseball." *Baseball Digest*, 1981.

Goldstein, Richard. *Spartan Seasons: How Baseball Survived the Second World War.* New York: Macmillan, 1980.

Halberstam, David. *Summer of '49.* New York: Morrow, 1989.

"Fielding Sensation." *Incabus* [Published in the Interest of Federal Employees], June 1949.

Montville, Leigh. *Ted Williams: The Biography of an American Hero.* New York: Doubleday, 2004.

Sherrod, Blackie. "The Jumble of Numbers, or Tall Tales" [Interview with Bobby Bragan]. *Dallas Morning News*, April 13, 1988.

Sherrod, Robert. *History of Marine Corps Aviation in World War II.* San Rafael, CA: Presidio Press, 1952.

Thorn, John and Pete Palmer, editors. *Total Baseball.* New York: Warner Books, 1989.